GOVERNMENT OF INDIA

ARMY DEPARTMENT

DRESS REGULATIONS
(INDIA)

1931

First published by
The Government of India Publications Branch
Calcutta.

Government of India Publications are obtainable from the Government of India Central Publication Branch, 3, Government Place, West, Calcutta, and from the following Agents :—

EUROPE.

OFFICE OF THE HIGH COMMISSIONER FOR INDIA, India House, Aldwych, LONDON, W. C. 2.
And at all Booksellers.

INDIA AND CEYLON : Provincial Book Depots.

MADRAS :—Superintendent, Government Press, Mount Road, Madras.
BOMBAY :—Superintendent, Government Printing and Stationery, Queen's Road, Bombay.
SIND :—Library attached to the Office of the Commissioner in Sind, Karachi.
BENGAL :—Bengal Secretariat Book Depôt, Writers' Buildings, Room No. 1, Ground Floor, Calcutta.
UNITED PROVINCES OF AGRA AND OUDH :—Superintendent of Government Press, United Provinces of Agra and Oudh, Allahabad.
PUNJAB :—Superintendent, Government Printing, Punjab, Lahore.
BURMA :—Superintendent, Government Printing, Burma, Rangoon.
CENTRAL PROVINCES AND BERAR :—Superintendent, Government Printing, Central Provinces, Nagpur.
ASSAM :—Superintendent, Assam Secretariat Press, Shillong.
BIHAR AND ORISSA :—Superintendent, Government Printing, Bihar and Orissa, P. O. Gulzarbagh, Patna.
NORTH-WEST FRONTIER PROVINCE :—Manager, Government Printing and Stationery, Peshawar.

Thacker, Spink & Co., Ltd., Calcutta and Simla.
W. Newman & Co., Ltd., Calcutta.
S. K. Lahiri & Co., Calcutta.
The Indian School Supply Depôt, 309, Bow Bazar Street, Calcutta.
Butterworth & Co. (India), Ltd., Calcutta.
M. C. Sarcar & Sons, 15, College Square, Calcutta.
Standard Literature Company, Limited, Calcutta.
Association Press, Calcutta.
Chukervertty, Chatterjee & Co., Ltd., 13, College Square, Calcutta.
The Book Company, Calcutta.
James Murray & Co., 12, Government Place, Calcutta. (For Meteorological Publications only.)
Ray Chaudhury & Co., 68-5, Ashutosh Mukherji Road, Calcutta.
Scientific Publishing Co., 9, Taltola Lane, Calcutta.
Chatterjee & Co., 3-1, Bacharam Chatterjee Lane, Calcutta.
Standard Law Book Society, 8-2, Hastings Street, Calcutta.
The Hindu Library, 3, Nandalal Mullick Lane, Calcutta.
Kamala Book Depôt, Ltd., 15, College Square, Calcutta.
*Bengal Flying Club, Dum Dum Cantt.
Kali Charan & Co., Municipal Market, Calcutta.
N. M. Roy Chowdhury & Co., 11, College Sqr., Calcutta.
B. C. Basak, Esq., Proprietor, Albert Library, Dacca.
Higginbothams, Madras.
Rochouse and Sons, Madras.
G. A. Nateson & Co., Publishers, George Town, Madras.
P. Varadachary & Co., Madras.
City Book Co., Madras.
Law Publishing Co., Mylapore, Madras.
The Booklover's Resort, Taikad, Trivandrum, South India.
E. M. Gopalakrishna Kone, Pudumandapam, Madura.
Central Book Depot, Madura.
Vijapur & Co., Vizagapatam.
Thacker & Co., Ltd., Bombay.
D. B. Taraporevala, Sons & Co., Bombay.
Ram Chandra Govind & Sons, Kalbadevi Road, Bombay.
N. M. Tripathi & Co., Booksellers, Princess Street, Kalbadevi Road, Bombay.
New and Secondhand Bookshop, Kalbadevi Road, Bombay.
J. M. Pandia & Co., Bombay.
A. H. Wheeler & Co., Allahabad, Calcutta and Bombay.
Bombay Book Depôt, Girgaon, Bombay.
Bennett, Coleman & Co., Ltd., The Times of India Press, Bombay.
The Popular Book Depôt, Bombay.
The Manager, Oriental Book Supplying Agency, 15, Shukrawar, Poona City.
Rama Krinash Bros., Opposite Bishrambag, Poona City.
S. P. Bookstall, 21, Budhwar, Poona.
Mangaldas & Sons, Booksellers and Publishers, Bhaga Talao, Surat.
The Standard Book and Stationery Co., 32-33, Arbab Road, Peshawar.
The Students Own Book Depot, Dharwar.

Shri Shankar Karnataka Pustaka Bhandara Malamuddi, Dharwar.
The Standard Bookstall, Karachi, Quetta, Delhi, Murree and Rawalpindi.
Frontier Book & Stationery Co., Rawalpindi.
*Hossenbhoy Karimji and Sons, Karachi.
The English Bookstall, Karachi.
Rose & Co., Karachi.
The Standard Bookstall, Quetta.
U. P. Malhotra & Co., Quetta.
J. Ray & Sons, 43, K. & L., Edwardes Road, Rawalpindi, Murree and Lahore.
The Standard Bookstall, Lahore, Nainital, Mussoorie, Dalhousie, Ambala Cantonment and Delhi.
The North India Christian Tract and Book Society, 18, Clive Road, Allahabad.
Ram Narain Lal, Katra, Allahabad.
"The Leader," Allahabad.
The Indian Army Book Depôt, Dayalbagh, Agra.
The English Book Depôt, Taj Road, Agra.
Gaya Prasad & Sons, Agra.
Narain & Co., Meston Road, Cawnpore.
The Indian Army Book Depôt, Jullundur City, Daryaganj, Delhi.
Manager, Newal Kishore Press, Lucknow.
The Upper India Publishing House Ltd., Literature Palace, Ammuddaula Park, Lucknow.
Rai Sahib M. Gulab Singh & Sons, Mufid-I-Am Press, Lahore and Allahabad.
Rama Krishna & Sons, Booksellers, Anarkali, Lahore.
Students Popular Depôt, Anarkali, Lahore.
The Standard Bookstall, Lahore.
The Proprietor, Punjab Sanskrit Book Depot Saidmitha Street, Lahore.
The Insurance Publicity Co., Ltd., Lahore.
The Punjab Religious Book Society, Lahore.
The Commercial Book Co., Lahore.
The University Book Agency, Karachi Road, Lahore.
Manager of the Imperial Book Depôt, 63, Chandni Chowk Street, Delhi.
J. M. Jaina & Bros., Delhi.
Fono Book Agency, New Delhi and Simla.
Oxford Book and Stationery Company, Delhi, Lahore, Simla, Meerut and Calcutta.
Supdt., American Baptist Mission Press, Rangoon.
Burma Book Club, Ltd., Rangoon.
S. C. Talukdar, Proprietor, Students & Co., Cooch Behar.
The Manager, The Indian Book Shop, Benares City.
Nandkishore & Bros., Chowk, Benares City.
The Srivilliputtur Co-operative Trading Union, Ltd., Srivilliputtur (S. I. R.).
Raghunath Prasad & Sons, Patna City.
The Students' Emporium, Patna.
K. L. Mathur & Bros., Guzri, Patna City.
Kamala Book Stores, Bankipore, Patna.
G. Banerjea and Bros., Ranchi.
M. C. Kothari, Raipura Road, Baroda.
B. Parikh & Co., Baroda.
The Hyderabad Book Depôt, Chaderghat, Hyderabad (Deccan).
S. Krishnaswamy & Co., Teppakulam P.O., Trichinopoly Fort.
Karnataka Publishing House, Bangalore City.
Bheema Sons, Fort, Bangalore City.
Superintendent, Bangalore Press, Lake View, Mysore Road, Bangalore City.

AGENT IN PALESTINE :—Steimatzky, Jerusalem.
* Agent for publications on aviation only.

REGISTER OF CORRECTIONS.

Year.	Clause and month.	Initials of person by whom corrected and date of correction.	Year.	Clause and month.	Initials of person by whom corrected and date of correction.

REGISTER OF CORRECTIONS.

Year.	Clause and month.	Initials of person by whom corrected and date of correction.	Year.	Clause and month.	Initials of person by whom corrected and date of correction.

PREFACE.

THIS volume contains the orders of the Government of India on the dress of the army in India and is to be read in conjunction with Dress Regulations for the Army (made applicable to the British services on the Indian establishment by India Army Order 448 of 1912), and the King's Regulations.

General or other officers commanding will be held responsible that no deviations from the authorized patterns in the uniform of officers, warrant officers and soldiers, nor mixed orders of dress, are permitted in their commands.

This publication has been corrected up to 1st November 1931.

G. M. YOUNG,
Secretary to the Government of India,
Army Department.

SIMLA.

APPENDICES.

	PAGE.
Appendix I.—Description of the " Sam Browne " belt, the web sword belt, the sword knot, and the web belt and bridle leather straps for carrying the greatcoat	63
Appendix II.—Description of the service Mark VI Webley pistol	64
Appendix III.—Description of shoulder chains	64
Appendix IV.—Descriptions of swords and scabbards worn by Indian army officers	64—68
Appendix V.—Description of the service water bottle	68
Appendix VI.—Details of certain orders of dress for warrant officers.	68
Appendix VII.—List of units whose officers are permitted to wear boots, leggings and putties which differ from the authorised patterns or colours	69
Appendix VIII.—Details of mess dress of Indian cavalry units	70—77
Appendix IX.—Details of badges and buttons for Indian cavalry units	78—83
Appendix X.—Details of mess dress for Indian pioneer and infantry units	84—99
Appendix XI.—Details of badges and buttons for Indian pioneer and infantry units	100—113
Appendix XII.—List of units who have been permitted to adopt a hot weather mess kit which differs from the standard pattern	114

DRESS REGULATIONS
(INDIA)

GENERAL INSTRUCTIONS.

1. Commanding officers are forbidden to introduce or to sanction any deviation from the sealed patterns of dress, clothing, equipment and badges. They will be responsible for replacing or restoring to the approved pattern any articles worn in their units which may be found not to be in conformity therewith.

2. They will however permit individual officers to continue to wear articles of dress already in their use which become obsolete by change of pattern in regulations. No permission to continue the wear of obsolete articles will extend beyond five years from the change of regulations, such articles may not be renewed, but must be replaced by the latest patterns.

3. The articles described in the following paragraphs are of universal application and will be worn by officers of all units, corps and departments. When obtaining uniform and equipment, officers should make sure, by personal comparison, if possible, that articles are being supplied according to sealed pattern.

4. No unauthorised ornament or emblem is to be worn in uniform, but special emblems may be carried on the headdress on anniversaries, provided authority has been obtained.

Units are authorised to wear the national flower or emblem in their headdress on the days specified:

St. George's Day.	English units.
St. Andrew's Day.	Scottish units.
St. David's Day.	Welsh units.
St. Patrick's Day.	Irish units.

These emblems may also be worn by English, Irish, Scottish and Welsh soldiers serving in other units.

All ranks, when not on duty, are authorized to wear a poppy on the uniform headdress on 11th November, being the anniversary of Armistice Day of the Great War.

5. Officers on leave are to be in possession of uniform for use if detailed for duty. Officers while in foreign countries are not to wear uniform without having obtained the permission of His Majesty's representative which will only be granted when they are employed on duty, or attending court, or at State ceremonies to which they have been invited. Permission to wear uniform at foreign manœuvres can only be obtained from the War Office.

6. Regulation uniform must not be worn at fancy dress balls, but there is no objection to military uniform of obsolete pattern being worn on such occasions.

7. Uniform will be worn while on duty.

8. Officers attending as spectators on occasions when troops parade under arms will wear the same order of dress as the troops but will not wear orders, decorations and medals.

8-A. When a general officer, who is a colonel of a regiment, officiates in a regimental capacity, it is a matter for his personal discretion whether he wears the uniform of his rank, or alternatively regimental uniform with the rank badges of a colonel. The rank badges of a general officer will not be worn with regimental uniform, nor the rank badges of a colonel with the uniform of a general officer.

9. Where any differences exist between the Home and Indian dress regulations, the articles of uniform authorised by the latter are not to be worn by officers of the British service after leaving the Indian establishment.

10. Details of full dress uniform have not been embodied in these regulations, but full dress of the patterns authorised for wear prior to August 1914 may be worn by officers who may be in possession of it, when not on duty with troops.

DETAILS OF DRESS AND UNIFORM.

11. **Aiguillette.**—The aiguillette is the distinguishing mark of officers serving on the staff of the army and in personal appointments. See para. 116.

For description and method of wearing it, see para. 107.

The aiguillette for field marshals, personal appointments to the King and Royal Family is included in the description of their respective uniforms in Dress Regulations for the Army. That for personal appointments to the Viceroy and Governor General of India in the description of their uniform—paras. 91 to **102.**

12. **Armlets.**—These are worn by certain officers below the rank of major-general to denote staff, etc., appointments held by them (see R. A. I.). Armlets are $3\frac{1}{2}$ inches wide and the distinctive lettering will be in $\frac{3}{4}$ inch letters. They are worn on the right arm above the elbow and in service dress serge or khaki drill only. The various armlets are as shewn in para. 116.

General officers, brigadiers comanding brigades, and officers attached to the staff will not wear armlets.

Colonels commandant, brigadiers and substantive colonels holding appointments for which armlets are authorised whether at army, command, district or brigade headquarters, will wear such armlets with their distinctive letterings.

13. **Badges of rank.**—The rank of officers is shown by badges as under :—

Field Marshal.—Crossed batons on a wreath of laurel, with a crown above.

General.—Crossed sword and baton, with crown and star above.

Details of dress and uniform.

Lieutenant General.—Crossed sword and baton, with crown above.

Major-General.—Crossed sword and baton, with star above.

Brigadiers.—Crown and 3 stars below, the two lower stars side by side, point to point.

Colonel.—Crown and two stars below.

Lieutenant-Colonel.—Crown and one star below.

Major.—Crown.

Captain.—Three stars.

Lieutenant.—Two stars.

Second-Lieutenant.—One star.

Badges of rank, except when otherwise ordered, will be worn on all shoulder cords and shoulder straps. They will be in silver embroidery on gold shoulder cords and gold-laced shoulder straps, in gilt or gilding metal on plain cloth shoulder straps and in gold embroidery on the frock-coat. In regiments dressed in green, they will be bronze.

The crowns when laid on shoulder cords or shoulder straps are 1-inch broad and 1 inch in height; the stars are 1 inch between opposite points.

The batons forming part of the field marshal's badges will be in embroidery and crimson velvet. General officer's badges are worn in pairs, point of the sword to the front and edge of blade outwards or towards the arm. The sword is 2 inches long and the baton $\frac{1}{8}$ inch shorter.

Officers having brevet, local, temporary, acting or honorary rank wear the badges of that rank.

The rank of Indian officers and of I. M. D. and I. A. V. C. personnel ranking as such is shown by metal badges worn on the shoulder straps as under :—

Risaldar major and subadar major.—Crown.

Risaldar and subadar.—Two stars.

Jemadar.—One star.

14. **Badges.**—No badges are allowed to be worn, except those authorised by these and the Dress Regulations for the Army. Civil insignia, chains and badges are not to be worn with military uniform.

Collar badges will be fixed with the centre of the badge 2 inches from the opening of the collar of the tunic or frock-coat. They may also be worn on the lapel of the mess jacket and above the step on the service dress jacket, where authorised. When worn on the former they will be placed three quarters of an inch below the medals.

15. **Badges, special.**—Regimental badges, devices and other distinctions granted under special authority are to be strictly preserved. Badges are to be metal unless otherwise ordered.

16. **Belts sword.**—As described for the respective services. They will be worn as follows :—

"(1) *British service.*—Under the tunic or dress jacket by all mounted officers (except those of Highland and Scottish regiments—including Scottish Rifles) and by all officers of rifle regiments (excluding Scottish Rifles) ; over the tunic or doublet by all other officers.

Over the frock-coat and under patrol jackets.

The web belt, described in Appendix I (*b*) will be worn by all officers who wear the sword belt under the tunic or patrol jacket, and with the frock-coat under the girdle or waist sash.

(2) *Indian Army and Indian Medical Service.*—The web sword belt, described in Appendix I (*b*), will be worn under the tunic or patrol jacket, and over the frock-coat or frock, drill khaki (under the sash or girdle) by all officers for whom it is the prescribed full dress belt. Infantry officers carrying colours wear the web sword belt over the tunic and under the sash.

Other full dress sword-belts will be worn over the tunic, frock-coat or frock, drill, khaki.

The web sword belt will be worn under serge frocks by officers of all branches of the service. Slings will be fitted with studs and holes so that they can be removed from the belt. At balls and entertainments when the sword is allowed to be taken off, officers who wear the belt over the tunic will continue to wear sword belt and slings ; other officers will remove them."

17. **Belts "Sam Browne."**—The universal pattern, "Sam Browne," in brown (or black) leather, with one or two braces, pistol case, ammunition pouch, frog and brown (or black) leather scabbard is worn with service dress. The frog will only be worn when the sword is worn.

On field service web equipment similar in pattern to that worn by the men, may be worn instead of the "Sam Browne" belt.

Officers of Indian regiments whose mess dress is rifle-green may adopt the black "Sam Browne" belt, etc., with white metal fittings provided all officers are dressed alike.

Officers of Indian regiments whose mess dress is drab (also the 10th Baluch Regiment) may adopt the brown "Sam Browne," belt with white metal fittings, under similar conditions.

BOOTS.

18. (*a*) *Full dress—mounted.*—Except where otherwise specified, black butcher boots will be worn. The height of the boot will vary according to the length of the leg. It should reach to about 4 inches from the top of the knee. The leg of the boot should be jacked sufficiently to prevent it from sinking. A spur rest is fixed 2 inches above the top edge of the heel to keep the spur horizontal.

(*b*) *Full dress—dismounted and undress.*—All officers will wear black Wellington boots, except in Highland regiments when black shoes will be worn with the kilt.

(c) *Full dress—levees and courts.*—Field-Marshals will wear black jacked boots, other officers as in (b) above.

(d) *Mess order.*—As in (b) above.

(e) *Service dress.*—Field-marshals; general officers; brigadiers; substantive colonels; staff officers not belonging to a regiment or corps; officers of cavalry; Royal Artillery officers in mechanized, pack and coast defence units on ceremonial occasions; Royal Artillery officers of horsed units; officers of the Indian Signal Corps, officers of the Royal Army Veterinary Corps, Indian Army Service Corps and Military Farms Department will wear brown field boots.

Royal Artillery officers in mechanized, pack and coast defence units on other than ceremonial occasions, and dismounted officers will wear brown ankle boots and putties. Officers of Highland regiments will wear brown shoes.

Mounted officers other than those referred to above and officers of the Indian Army Ordnance Corps will wear brown ankle boots and leggings.

"(NOTE.—I. A. S. C. Officers with mechanized units will wear field boots on ceremonial parades and inspections. On all other parades they will wear putties and brown ankle boots)."

Staff officers belonging to a regiment or corps will wear the footwear prescribed for mounted officers of their unit, but those in possession of field boots may continue to wear them.

The brown ankle boot has a plain toe-cap, *i.e.*, without any ornamental piercing or stitching.

The brown field boot has a soft leg, stiffened to a depth of 4 to 6 inches from the top, laced at the instep with 7 to 9 pairs of eyelet holes, plain toe-cap, horizontal counter in line with the third lace hole from the bottom and $3\frac{1}{4}$-inches above the top of the heel, a leather garter at the top of the leg. The number of pairs of eyelet holes between 7 and 9, the provision of spur rests and a gusset with a strap and buckle at the top of the boot is optional.

The wearing of canvas gaiters is prohibited.

Units, whose officers are permitted to wear boots, leggings and putties which differ from the standard pattern or colour, are shewn in Appendix VII.

19. **Buttons.**—Buttons are of the following sizes and are used as shewn :—

Large (Gilding metal) 35 to 40 lines .	For the front of serge jackets, great coats and coats warm.
Small (Gilding metal) 24 to 34 lines .	For the fronts of undress serge frocks and khaki drill jackets.
	For the pockets of undress serge frocks, serge and khaki drill jackets.
	For the cuffs of all garments when authorised.
	For fastening the shoulder straps of all garments so fitted.
	For the fronts of mess jackets when authorised.
Cap (Gilding metal) 20 lines . .	For caps.
Vest and gorget (Gilt) 20 lines . .	For mess vests and gorget patches.

Service Dress Serge.

20. **Breeches Bedford cord.**—Staff officers, officers of mounted units, and mounted officers of dismounted units—drab coloured Bedford cord or cavalry

twill with drab coloured buckskin strappings; a small horn button about $2\frac{1}{2}$ inches from bottom of each leg at the back for leggings or field boot to be attached, to reach about 6 inches below the knee, fairly loose over hip and thigh with a good fullness at top half over the knee. Openings at bottom of legs about 5 inches long with eyelet-holes for laces on either side, the top and bottom eyelet-holes being about $\frac{1}{2}$ inch from top and bottom of opening, the other holes being equidistant, fly front, two cross pockets, buckle and strap at the back.

It is optional for button-holes and buttons to be substituted for eyelet-holes and laces, but all officers of a unit for whom these breeches are authorized must wear the same pattern.

21. **Breeches, knickerbocker.**—Officers of dismounted services, except those of Highland regiments who wear the kilt. Drab material to match the service dress jacket; cut fairly loose round the hips; continuations of same material about three inches deep which may at option be fastened with buttons and button-holes or with a strap and buckle. Any superfluous material at the bottom should be fulled on all round when seaming on the continuations. The fall over at the knee must not exceed four inches; fly fronts, the top button being on the inside of fly while the button-hole for same is just behind the button catch seam. Two side pockets; buckle and strap at back; waist lining of drab flannel.

Service Dress, Drill.

22. **Breeches, cord, khaki or khaki drill.**—Cord khaki or khaki drill of the authorised shade of the pattern described in para. 20, with strappings of the same material as the breeches.

23. **Breeches, knickerbockers, khaki drill.**—Khaki drill of the authorised shade of the pattern described in para. 21.

Breeches, khaki, drill, (para. 22) may be worn with khaki drill uniform by officers of the Indian army provided all officers of a unit are dressed alike.

Shorts may be worn at the option of regiments under the conditions laid down in para. 47.

Khaki Jodhpur breeches with ankle boots (or shoes) without spurs may be worn by officers in barracks when not on parade with troops.

24. **Cap-comforter.**—Brown silk, similar to the pattern for rank and file.

25. **Cap, field.**—Regimental pattern, may be worn in camp, on service, and at manœuvres. Its upkeep is optional.

26. **Cap forage, universal pattern.**—Worn with cover (para. 28) by general officers, brigadiers, substantive colonels and Indian Army officers.

Substantive colonels in command of units of the Indian Army will wear the forage cap as worn by British officers of their units.

Cloth, with three welts, $4\frac{1}{4}$ inches total depth, diameter across the top $10\frac{3}{8}$ inches for a cap fitting $21\frac{3}{4}$ inches in circumference, the top to be $\frac{1}{8}$ inch larger or smaller in diameter for every $\frac{1}{4}$ inch the cap may vary in size of head above or below the before-mentioned standard, e.g., a cap $22\frac{1}{4}$ inches in

Details of dress and uniform. 7

circumference, diameter across the top $10\frac{5}{8}$ inches; cap 21 inches in circumference, diameter 10 inches. The sides to be made in four pieces, and to be $2\frac{1}{8}$ inches deep between the welts, a cloth band $1\frac{1}{2}$ inches wide placed between the two lower welts.

The cap set up on a band of stiff leather, or other material, $1\frac{3}{4}$ inches deep, but not stiffened up in front.

Chin-strap of black patent leather $\frac{3}{8}$ inch wide, buttoned on to two "cap" gilt buttons placed immediately behind the corners of the peak.

The peak to droop at an angle of 45 degrees and to be 2 inches deep in the middle when worn with embroidery, and $1\frac{3}{4}$ inches when plain.

Peaks will be embroidered as follows :—

Field Marshals and general officers.—Two rows of oak-leaf embroidery.

Brigadiers, substantive colonels.—One row of oak leaf embroidery on lower edge.

Other field officers.—Plain gold embroidery $\frac{3}{4}$ inch wide, on lower edge.

Field officers of rifle regiments and Indian infantry dressed in green or drab.—Black or drab oak leaf embroidery on lower edge.

Other officers.—Plain peak.

27. **Cap, service dress.**—(a) Stiff pattern, of the same shape as the forage cap (para. 25) but of drab material to match the service dress; brown leather chinstrap; two bronze buttons. (b) Soft pattern, of the same shape as the stiff pattern, but with a flexible peak, and not wired round the top of the cap.

The soft pattern cap (and the Tam O'Shanter in Scottish regiments), is carried or worn on active service, at training and on manœuvres.

The cap, service dress, is optional for officers of the Indian army.

28. **Covers to forage caps.**—These will cover the top of the cap only, the distinctive band, the peak and the badge being left uncovered.

When a blue or other coloured forage cap is worn in service dress (khaki drill or serge), a khaki or drab cover will be used.

The blue or other coloured forage cap (without khaki cover) will be worn with mess dress and with the blue serge frock.

A white cap cover may be worn with the blue or other coloured forage cap in mess dress or with the blue serge frock, provided that all officers of a unit and staffs are dressed alike in this respect.

28-A. **Coat, British, Warm.**—Cut double breasted and to reach to the knee, a slit at centre of back, turn down collar two inches deep with lapel and step; three large leather buttons on each side to show, and a bone button under turn; two small leather buttons on cuffs with $3\frac{1}{2}$-inch slit, two bottom pockets with flap, one inside breast; a sword slit on the left side seam; shoulder straps of the same material as garment fastened with a small bone button under collar. Badges of rank in gilt metal; the edges are single stitched; a tab under collar to button across when required.

This coat is the approved pattern for wear in service dress by general officers and substantive colonels, also by officers of the Household Cavalry and Foot Guards except as provided in para. 36.

For officers below the rank of substantive colonels (except as mentioned above), it is an optional garment for wear when not parading with troops.

For general officers, brigadiers and substantive colonels the material is of Angola cloth of a light drab colour approximating to that of the alternative shade of the breeches, mounted pattern.

In other cases the material and colour is left to the discretion of regiments and corps except that the shade will be either the approved shade for service dress garments or the alternative shade of the mounted pattern breeches. All officers of a unit must be dressed alike.

29. **Collars.**—The pattern is left to the discretion of commanding officers but all officers of a unit must be dressed alike.

Drab flannel or khaki cotton collars will be worn with the service dress and khaki drill jackets at all times. A plain gold safety pin may be worn under the tie to keep the soft collar in place.

30. **Frock-coat, universal.**—Blue cloth, double breasted, with stand-up collar; plain sleeves with two small buttons and button holes at the bottom; two rows of large regimental buttons down the front, six in each row at equal distances, the distance between the rows 8 inches at the top and $4\frac{1}{2}$ inches at the bottom, (*these measurements will not be exceeded*); flaps behind 10 inches deep, one button on each flap and one on each side of the waist; the skirt to reach to the knees and to be lined; shoulder-straps of cloth the same material as the garment attached by an under-piece passed through a loop on the lower part of the shoulder, fastened at the top by a small button which passes through both under-piece and shoulder-strap; the top of the strap is triangular. Collar badges according to unit. Badges of rank in gold embroidery, on shoulder straps.

In the Indian army this garment, is only worn by general officers, for whom it is obligatory, and staff officers, for whom it is optional.

31. **Frock serge.**—Blue angola, tartan or serge according to climate, full in chest, cut with broad back slits at sides, five small buttons down the front, length of skirt as for tunic. Two breast patch pockets outside, $6\frac{3}{4}$ inche wide, 8 inches deep, the top edge of pocket in line with the second button, three-pointed flap, small button, and hole, loose plait on rear side of pocket, two similar outside patch pockets below, with three-pointed flap. Two inside breast pockets up and down with hole and button, two inside skirt pockets, with hole and button. Black alpaca lining. Shoulder straps of same material as the frock, fastened with a small button. Stand-up collar from $1\frac{1}{4}$ to $1\frac{3}{4}$ inches high. Sleeves with pointed cuffs 6 inches high, with $2\frac{1}{4}$ inch slit, two small buttons and button holes. Badges of rank in metal. No collar badges.

In regiments dressed in green the frock will be dark green, and in Highland and Scottish regiments the front of the skirt will be rounded off to Highland pattern.

Details of dress and uniform.

32. Officers in possession of the serge frock with open front and turn down collar will be permitted to continue it in wear until requiring replacement, but all future provision will be of the pattern laid down in para. 31 above.

33. **Gloves,** *Full dress.*—White doeskin or buckskin. For Indian infantry regiments dressed in green-black; dressed in drab-brown or drab leather.

Service dress.—Brown or buff wash leather. All officers of a regiment will be dressed alike.

White gloves will always be worn when attending dances in mess kit.

34. **Gorget patches.**—Officers of the rank of substantive colonel and above, except substantive colonels serving with units of the Indian army will wear gorget patches as noted below on the collar of the serge frock, and serge service dress and khaki drill jackets.

The gorget patches will be $3\frac{1}{2}$ inches in length and $1\frac{1}{4}$ inches wide, triangular at the points and shaped to fit the collar above the step.

(a) **For Field-Marshals and general officers.**

(i) Except as stated below: scarlet cloth.

Exceptions are :—

(ii) Medical Services; black velvet.

(iii) Army Veterinary Service: maroon cloth.

(iv) Chaplain General and chaplains with relative rank as generals: purple cloth.

In each case the gorget patch will have a line of gold oak leaf embroidery down the centre and a small gorget button.

(b) **For brigadiers substantive colonels.**

(i) Except as stated below: scarlet cloth.

Exceptions are :—

(ii) R.A.M.C., dull cherry cloth

(iii) I.M.S., black velvet.

(iv) Army Veterinary Service: maroon cloth.

(v) Chaplains with relative rank as colonels on the staff or substantive colonels: purple cloth.

In each case the gorget patch will have a line of silk gimp of the colour of the cloth down the centre and a small gorget button.

35. **Greatcoat, universal pattern.**—Cloth, drab mixture, milled and water-proofed; of sealed pattern, cut and shade; double breasted, to reach within a foot of the ground; stand and fall collar 5 inches deep (2-inch stand and 3-inch fall), fastening with two hooks and eyes; cloth tab and buttons; a $2\frac{1}{4}$-inch inverted expanding pleat down the centre of the back, from the

collar to the waist terminating under the back strap; sleeves with loose turn back cuffs of single material, 6 inches deep; two large cross pockets with slightly curved flaps at the waist in front; vertical slit for sword jetted in left side $1\frac{1}{2}$ inches above the pocket; a pocket in the left breast placed vertically between the second and third button; two rows of buttons down the front, four in each row, about $6\frac{1}{2}$ inches apart, the rows 8 inches apart at the top and 4 inches at the bottom; two buttons to back slit with holes in a fly; a 2-inch cloth back strap sewn in side seams fastened with three holes and buttons; skirt to fasten with two tabs and buttons inside, and to run squarely all round; coat lined to the waist only; shoulder straps of same material as the garment, sewn on to the shoulder at base and fastened at the top by a small button; the top of the strap is triangular. Buttons and badges rank in gilt metal, except of for rifle regiments and Royal Army Chaplains Department.

The coat is cut below the waist with spring to form 8-inch lap, or 4 inches on from the centre line. The slit at the back should be of suitable length for riding.

This coat is the approved pattern for wear by all officers below the rank of substantive colonel except for officers of the Household Cavalry and Foot Guards.

Officers in possession of the great coat previously authorised may continue to wear it until replacement becomes necessary.

36. **Greatcoat for general officers and substantive colonels.**—Atholl grey milled cloth, double breasted, 2 cross pockets, pivot sleeves, 6 buttons on either side, 8 to 10 inches apart at the top and 4 to 6 inches at the bottom, lined with scarlet ratinet. Plain cloth shoulder straps fastened with a small button. Sword slit and flap at side. There is no objection to generals and colonels continuing to wear the drab greatcoats if in their possession, but on the occasions when full dress is worn and a greatcoat is necessary, it should be that prescribed for their rank, *viz.*, Atholl grey.

37. **Cape.**—Of similar material to the greatcoat, of sufficient length to afford protection to the knees when mounted. Turndown collar 3 inches in depth, unlined, fastened with two hooks and eyes at the collar and 5 buttons down the front. The cape is for wear as a separate garment.

38. **Helmet, khaki.**—"Wolseley" pattern, cork, made with six seams, bound with buff leather; projecting brim all round, 3 inches in front, 4 inches at back, 2 inches at sides; ventilated at top with zinc button covered with khaki drill; side hooks. At top of helmet, a collet riveted on to a collar $\frac{3}{8}$ inch wide to receive the button. Brown or black leather chinstrap $\frac{3}{8}$ inch wide. A plain khaki pagri.

British officers serving with Indian units may wear a lungi in the place of a helmet with khaki dress. All officers of a unit will be dressed alike.

Patches or flashes, hackles, etc., may be worn on the helmet by officers of the British service and Indian army, provided that all officers of a regiment, corps, etc., are dressed alike. Such permission extends to British units whilst serving within Indian limits or on the Indian establishment.

Details of dress and uniform.

Wolseley helmets will be worn by officers on all occasions except that pith hats of universal pattern may be worn as follows (provided that all officers of a regiment, corps, etc., are dressed alike) :—

(a) When British other ranks are authorised by competent authority to wear pith hats.

(b) Officer instructors and students of the Royal Tank School when on training parades which necessitate work inside a mechanically propelled vehicle.

(c) Officer students at the Equitation School.

(d) British officers of the Indian army may wear the service pattern pith hat, or Cawnpore Tent Club pattern (with quilted cover and no pagri), on all parades and duties, other than ceremonial parades.

39. **Jacket service dress—universal pattern.**—Khaki drill of the authorised shade, single-breasted, cut as a lounge coat with back seams, very loose at the chest and shoulders but fitted at the waist and cut straight fronted. Step collar, depth of opening about 3 inches, two cross-patch breast pockets, above, $6\frac{1}{2}$ inches wide and $7\frac{1}{2}$ inches deep to the top of the flap, box plait in centre $2\frac{1}{4}$ inches wide, three pointed flap $6\frac{1}{2}$ inches wide and $2\frac{1}{4}$ inches deep, two expanding pockets below the waist at the sides, $9\frac{1}{4}$ inches wide at the top and $10\frac{1}{2}$ inches at the bottom, 8 inches deep to the top of the pocket and fastened at the top with a small button, flap with button-hole to cover pocket $3\frac{1}{4}$ inches deep, $10\frac{3}{4}$ inches wide. The top of the pockets sewn down at the corners in such a manner that on service the pocket can be expanded at the top also ; inside watch pocket with tab above for chain or strap. Four large (Indian army-small) regimental buttons down the front, the bottom one to show just below the lower edge of the belt when worn. Cuffs pointed. Shoulder straps of same material as the jacket, fastened with a small regimental button. Badges of rank in metal.

In Highland and Scottish regiments the skirts of the jackets are rounded off to follow the natural line instead of being cut in below the bottom button.

40. **Jacket, service dress (serge).**—Drab winter serge of the pattern described above.

This jacket will only be worn by officers off parade or when parading with troops wearing drab serge uniform.

Collar badges are worn on the collar above the step by officers of services for which collar badges are authorised, except by officers of and above the rank of substantive colonel for whom gorget patches are authorised (see para. 34).

British and Indian officers of Indian cavalry, Indian Light and Mountain Artillery and Indian infantry may wear at their option a khaki frock on parade with their men of a similar pattern to that worn by the rank and file. All officers of a unit will be dressed alike.

41. **Leggings.**—Black or brown leather fastening up the front with laces and six hooks. The hooks are placed on the outer flap. See para. 18 (e) and Appendix VII.

42. **Mourning.**—When attending military funerals or memorial services connected therewith, officers and warrant officers will wear a mourning band of black crape, $3\frac{1}{4}$ inches wide, round the left arm above the elbow. It will not be worn at levees or at Court, except when the Court is in mourning, nor will it be worn at ceremonies such as the unveiling of memorials and Armistice Day celebrations.

An officer or warrant officer in private mounring may, when in uniform, wear a mourning band as described above.

43. **Putties.**—Woollen, to match the colour of the service dress serge or khaki drill. (See para. 18 (*e*).) Units whose officers are allowed to wear putties of a colour other than khaki are shown in Appendix VII.

44. **Saddlery.**—As laid down in the equipment regulations.

45. **Service dress.**—For the British service means drill or serge, and when either kind is referred to specifically, the term "drill" or "serge" will be added.

For Indian troops the only authorised service dress is khaki drill.

46. **Shirts.**—With cloth mess dress—white linen stiff fronted. With hot weather dress—soft fronted. Drab flannel or khaki cotton shirts will always be worn with service dress serge or khaki drill. Khaki shirts may be worn without the jacket, in which case shoulder straps and badges of rank will be provided. The collar of the shirt may then be worn open without a tie.

47. **Shorts.**—For dismounted officers as an optional garment in lieu of breeches (paras. 20 to 23). Khaki drill as for rank and file. Hose tops may be worn with shorts.

48. **Shoulder chains.**—Worn with full dress and in service dress when worn by the men. They will not be worn on tunics or frock-coats.

Shoulder chains may be worn by Indian cavalry (all ranks) with service dress when worn as full dress. The chains will be worn over the shoulder straps which will, under no circumstances, be removed.

49. **Shoulder cords or shoulder straps.**—Are worn on tunics, jackets, frock-coats, serge frocks and great-coats. Shoulder titles of the same pattern as worn by the men will be worn with service dress serge and khaki drill jackets.

50. **Spurs, steel.**—With butcher boots, field boots and ankle boots, hunting spurs of sealed pattern will be worn; with butcher boots, steel chains and black strap; with black ankle boots, black straps and shield (no chains); with brown field and ankle boots, brown straps and shield (no chains); with Wellington boots, box spurs with plain rowels.

Spurs will be worn in full dress and service dress by all general officers, staff officers, officers of mounted services, field officers and adjutants of all services and all officers permanently in command of companies of infantry.

They will also be worn in mess dress, undress and at levees and courts when Wellington boots are worn, by all the above mentioned officers.

Other officers whose duties require them to be mounted will not wear spurs in any order of dismounted dress, but will wear spurs and mounted kit when actually mounted.

Details of dress and uniform. 13

They will not be worn on board ship when travelling, or by officers inspecting armaments or magazines. They may be removed when dancing.

The new pattern hunting spur, steel, is made of stainless steel. The maximum length of the neck of the spur is $1\frac{1}{4}$ inches and the minimum length 1 inch; the sides of the neck are flat.

51. **Swords and scabbards.**—The pattern laid down for the arm of the service. Swords will be carried on parades and duties unless otherwise directed. They will not be worn on board ship, at mess, or at stables.

Swords will be carried on the saddle by mounted officers in all mounted "orders of dress" other than review order (full dress).

The scabbards of officers of dismounted units in review order (full dress) are to be hooked up by those who wear the waist belt over the tunic and carried in left hand by other officers.

The scabbard will be carried in the left hand by mounted officers when on dismounted duties.

52. **Sword knots.**—Worn loose in all orders of dress by mounted officers, viz., general officers, staff officers, officers of mounted services, field officers and adjutants of all services and officers permanently in command of companies of infantry. Other officers will wear the sword knot neatly coiled round the guard of the sword. (See App. I (c)).

53. **Ties.**—Black ties are worn with mess dress, except by officers of the Oxfordshire and Buckinghamshire Light Infantry who wear white ties. A drab tie tied in a sailor's knot will be worn with service dress serge and khaki drill jackets.

54. **Trousers and pantaloons.**—For mounted officers trousers or overalls are cut straight and from $1\frac{1}{2}$ to 2 inches longer than ordinary trousers. They will be strapped firmly down to the boot and fit closely above the spurs. In mess dress, overalls are worn by all officers.

Service dress trousers with ankle boots or shoes, will not be worn on parade or duty except at stables and on fatigue duties in barracks, or when employed in offices.

Pantaloons are cut loose in the thigh and tight at the knee. Ample length from the hip to the knee is essential so that the wearer can have the necessary freedom in mounting and dismounting. Buckskin strapping at the knee, and, if made for hard wear, seat strapping also.

Pantaloons should be furnished with a waist strap and buckle and with cross pockets.

55. **Waterproof coat.**—The provision of this garment is not compulsory, and it is not obligatory in any order of dress. It is not intended that any particular pattern should be rigidly followed, but it should be of drab coloured material.

56. **Whistles.**—There is no sealed pattern, but all the officers of a unit will carry the same pattern. They will be attached to a lanyard of regimental pattern and carried in the left breast pocket of the service dress jacket, in mounted services, when on duty with troops, in dismounted services when in marching drill order.

Alternatively the whistle may be carried attached to a stud or buckle on the shoulder belt of the Sam Browne belt.

All officers of a unit will be dressed alike.

57. Purchase of articles of clothing, etc.—Officers are permitted to purchase such articles of clothing, necessaries and materials suitable for their uniforms and equipment as may be available from clothing depots or arsenals or regimental stores.

The rules under which these issues can be made will be found in Clothing and Equipment Regulations.

ORDERS, DECORATIONS AND MEDALS.

58. Decorations and medals, except those mentioned below, are worn on the left breast. In full dress they are worn over the sash in Highland and Scottish regiments, and under the pouch belt when this is worn. They are to be worn in a horizontal line, suspended from a single bar of which no part is to be seen, or stitched to the garment, and placed midway between the first and second buttons from the bottom of the collar. In Hussar regiments they will be placed immediately below the top bar of lace on the left breast of the tunic.

Medals will be worn in the order laid down in para. 72.

Medals awarded by the Royal Humane Society or by the Royal National Lifeboat Institution will, when authorized, be worn in a position corresponding with war medals, on the right breast.

When the decorations and medals cannot, on account of their number, be suspended from the bar so as to be fully seen, they are to overlap.

Medals are to be worn so as to show the Sovereign's head.

The first earned clasp will be worn nearest the medal.

MINIATURE DECORATIONS AND MEDALS.

59. Miniature decorations and medals are worn with mess dress and with evening dress (plain clothes), see paras. 61 and 69.

Miniatures of orders, decorations and medals will be one half the size of the full size orders, decorations or medals, except that Knights Grand Cross, Knights Grand Commander, Knights Commander and Commanders or Companions will wear the miniatures laid down in the statutes of the respective orders.

The miniatures of companionship or membership of an order will not be removed when the broad riband, star, or badge is worn in evening dress (plain clothes), by a Knight Grand Cross, Knight Commander, etc.

WITH FULL DRESS.

60 (i). The riband of the Order of the Garter, also that of the Order of the Thistle, is worn over the *left* shoulder and under the waist sash, the badge resting on the right hip and the star affixed to the left breast.

The riband of the Order of St. Patrick is worn over the *right* shoulder and under the waist sash, the badge resting on the left hip, and the star affixed to the left breast.

(ii) The insignia of the 1st Class (Knight Grand Cross or Knight Grand Commander) are worn as follows :—

> (*a*) The broad riband over the right shoulder and under the waist sash, the bow from which the badge is suspended resting on the left hip, immediately below the belt or sash. Only one riband is worn.
>
> (*b*) Stars are worn on the left breast. When two stars are worn that of the senior order is placed directly above the other. Three stars are worn in triangular formation, and four stars are worn in a diamond formation. The star of the senior order is worn on top, except that in the case of three stars it is permissible for the two senior stars to be worn in line on top with the junior star beneath. Not more than four stars are worn at any one time.

(iii) The insignia of the 2nd Class (Knight Commander) are worn as follows. The riband with the badge attached is worn round the neck inside and under the collar of the uniform coat, so that the badge hangs outside about ¾ inch below the collar.

> (*a*) Where a Knight Commander is in possession of more than one riband and badge, the remainder will be worn one below the other, beginning about an inch below the senior badge, each suspended from a riband, emerging about ¾ inch between the buttons of the tunic. A small eye is stitched inside the tunic to which the riband is fastened by a hook. Not more than three neck badges will be worn at any one time.
>
> (*b*) Stars are worn on the left breast. The instructions in (ii) (*b*) above also apply to stars of Knights Commander.

(iv) The insignia of the 3rd Class (companion or commander) are ribands and badges worn round the neck. These are worn in the same manner as the ribands and badges of Knights Commander. See (iii) (*a*) above.

(v) Badges of a Companion of the Distinguished Service Order or badges of the 4th and 5th Class (officer or member) of an order are worn on the left breast in the position assigned to them.

(vi) For foreign decorations and medals see para. 74.

With Mess Dress.

61. Miniature badges of orders, decorations and medals will be worn with mess dress on the left lapel of the jacket (by the Household Cavalry on the left breast), in one horizontal line, one inch below the point of the shoulder, suspended from a bar of which no part is to be seen.

> (i) The length of the bar must vary with the number of miniatures, but in no case should it project beyond either the lapel or shoulder seam of the jacket. When the miniatures cannot, on account of their number, be suspended from the bar so as to be fully seen, they are to overlap.

(ii) Collar badges, when worn on the mess jacket, will be placed ¾ inch below the medals.

(iii) The insignia of the Order of the Garter, the Order of the Thistle, the Order of St. Patrick, the Order of Merit and the Order of Companion of Honour are not worn in miniature.

(iv) With mess dress, stars, ribands and badges (except the ribands and badges of the Order of Merit and of Companions of Honour) are not worn.

Knights Grand Cross, Knights Grand Commander, Knights Commander Commanders and Companions wear miniatures of their badges on the left breast, with other miniature decorations and medals.

With Service Dress.

62. The following instructions regarding the wearing of orders, decorations and medals with service dress uniform have been approved as a temporary measure—

Orders, decorations and medals will be worn in service dress uniform by officers on the following occasions :—

(a) At levees and at investitures at which levee dress is worn by all officers.

(b) At military funerals and memorial services connected therewith by all officers.

(c) On ceremonial parades. By officers when actually on parade with their unit or formations.*

Collars and broad ribands of orders (Knights Grand Cross and Knights Grand Commander) will not be worn with service dress.

Stars of orders.—Stars not exceeding two in number will be worn in line, on the left side, immediately below the medals.

Badges of orders worn round the neck.—Not more than two such badges will be worn. An officer in possession of one badge will wear it round the neck with the riband under the shirt collar and the badge over the tie ; an officer in possession of more than one badge will wear the badge of the senior order as above described, and that of the next senior order suspended from a riband emerging about ¾ inch immediately below the top button-hole of the jacket, a small eye being stitched inside the coat, to which the riband will be fastened by a hook.

Other orders, decorations and medals.—These will be worn in the prescribed order on the left breast.

For foreign decorations and medals see para. 124.

Position of medals.—The bar from which badges of orders, decorations or medals are suspended will be placed immediately above the left breast pocket of jackets with an open collar and the centre of the bar midway between the first and second buttons of jackets fitted with a stand up collar.

---

* Includes divisional and brigade commanders and their staffs when actually on parade with their formations.

Length of ribands.—When medals and decorations are worn on the breast the riband will be one inch in length, unless the possession of clasps necessitates its being longer. The uppermost clasp will be one-inch from the top of the riband. When two or more medals and decorations are worn they will be so arranged that the lower edges (or lowest point of a star) are in line. The lengths of all ribands will be regulated by that of the decoration or medal which, including clasps, is the longest. These instructions apply equally to miniature medals and decorations.

63. **Wearing of ribands without medals or decorations.**—The ribands will be ⅜ inch in length and will be worn on a bar or sewn on the jacket, without intervals, immediately above the left breast pocket of the jacket with an open collar, and the centre of the bar or ribbons midway between the first and second buttons of jackets fitted with a standup collar. When there is not sufficient room to wear the ribands in one row, they will be worn in two or more rows at convenient intervals, not more than ½ inch apart; the centre of the rows will occupy the position indicated above.

No riband will be covered by the lapel of the service dress jacket.

64. **Ribands of foreign orders, decorations and medals.**—The ribands of foreign orders, decorations and medals worn on service dress will be the plain riband of the order, decoration or medal, as the case may be, with the exception that those foreign orders that include a "rosette" on the riband of the badge or insignia of the order, in which case a "rosette" will also be worn on the small riband worn in service dress uniform.

Width of ribands of foreign orders and decorations worn with service dress.—The riband of a foreign order or decoration worn with service dress will in all cases be that of the grade or class which most closely conforms in width to that of the British medal riband, *i.e.*, as nearly as possible 1¼ inches.

65. **"Semi-knots" to be worn on the riband of the Legion of Honour.**—"Semi-knots" in addition to the rosette will be worn on the riband of the Legion of Honour in service dress by officers who have received the following classes of this decoration :—

Grand Cross. Two "Semi-knots" of gold riband.

Grand Officer. One "semi-knot" of gold and one of silver riband.

Commander. Two "semi-knots" of silver riband.

The gold and silver ribands of which the "semi-knots" are made are ¼ inch in width.

66. **Wearing of orders, decorations and medals in service dress by retired officers.** Retired officers of the regular and territorial army reserve of officers, officers who have resigned or relinquished their commissions with permission to retain rank, and officers who have been granted permission to wear uniform on special occasions are permitted to wear, on appropriate occasions, orders, decorations and medals with service dress uniform. The method of wearing orders and decorations is shown in para. 62.

67. **Emblems worn on ribands in "undress" and service dress to denote the possession of a bar or bars to certain decorations and medals.**—The following emblems are worn on the ribands of certain decorations and medals, when worn on "undress" and service dress garments, to denote that the wearer

has been awarded a bar or bars to the original decoration or medal for subsequent acts of bravery or for further distinguished conduct in the field :—

Victoria Cross.—A miniature replica of the Victoria Cross. The award of a bar to the original decoration will be marked by the addition of a second miniature Cross on the riband, an additional Cross being added for each bar awarded.

Distinguished Service Order .
Military Cross . . .
Distinguished Conduct Medal
Military Medal . . .
Medal for Meritorious Service
} A small silver rose ; one or more according to the number of bars awarded.

1914 Star . . . A small silver rose in the centre of the riband.

These emblems do not form part of the decoration or medal, and are not to be worn on the riband when the decoration or medal is worn in original on the full dress tunic or service dress jacket, or in miniature on the mess jacket.

68. **Wearing of emblem to denote the wearer has been mentioned in despatches.**—The emblem (an oak-leaf in bronze) is in two sizes and is worn on the *Victory medal* riband. (*a*) The larger size is attached to the riband when the medal is worn. It will be affixed to the small riband when the medal is not worn, transversely across the riband, stem to the right.

Additional emblems will not be worn in respect of a second or subsequent mention in despatches.

With evening dress.

69. The following are the occasions upon which orders, miniature decorations and medals are to be worn with evening dress, *viz.* :—

(i) At all parties and dinners when the members of the Royal Family referred to below are present :—

Their Majesties the King and Queen.

Their Royal Highnesses—

The Prince of Wales.

The Duke and Duchess of York

The Duke of Gloucester.

Prince George.

Princess Mary, Viscountess Lascelles.

Princess Victoria.

The Duke of Connaught.

Princess Louise, Duchess of Argyll.

Princess Beatrice.

Prince and Princess Arthur of Connaught.

Princess Alice, Countess of Athlone.

The host should notify his guests if any of these members of the Royal Family will be present.

(ii) At all parties and dinners given in houses of ambassadors and ministers accredited to the court, unless otherwise notified by the ambassador or minister concerned.

A decoration of the country concerned should be worn in preference to a British one, and if both are worn, the former should take precedence of the latter.

(iii) At all official dinners and receptions, including naval, military and air force dinners, dinners of city livery companies, and public dinners.

The word "Decorations" on the invitation card to be the intimation from the host that the entertainment is an official one.

(iv) On official occasions when entertained by :—

> The Lord Lieutenant of a county within his county.
> The High Sheriff of a county within his county.
> Cabinet ministers.
> Ex-cabinet ministers.
> Knights of the Order of the Garter.
> Knights of the Order of the Thistle.
> Knights of the Order of St. Patrick.
> Great officers of state and of the King's household.
> Lord mayors and mayors.
> Lord provosts and provosts.

The word "Decorations" on the invitation card to be the intimation from the host that the entertainment is an official one.

Nothing in the above shall affect in any way the practice of the Knights of the Orders of the Garter, Thistle and St. Patrick, and members of the Order of Merit, of wearing their insignia in accordance with ancient custom.

70. (a) The riband of the Order of the Garter and that of the Order of the Thistle are worn under the coat, as shown in para. 71 (a) (i) except that the riband will be fastened on the waistcoat at the front of the left armhole, the badge resting on the right hip, and the star being affixed to the left breast of the coat. The riband of the Order of St. Patrick will be worn in a similar manner, but fastened at the front of the right armhole, the badge resting on the left hip, and the star being affixed to the left breast of the coat.

(b) Knights Grand Cross and Knights Commanders on all occasions, when wearing the stars of their orders, will also wear a riband and badge.

One badge only is worn round the neck, and as a rule the senior badge is thus worn, unless a junior one should appear to be more appropriate to the occasion. The riband (preferably of miniature width) from which this badge is suspended, is worn under the white tie, the badge hanging about an inch below. All badges are worn also in miniature, with other decorations and medals, on the lapel of the coat.

71. (a) The insignia of the 1st Class (Knight Grand Cross or Knight Grand Commander) are worn as follows :—

    (i) The broad riband is worn on the waistcoat and does not pass over the shoulder and down the back as with the uniform coat. It is fastened at the front of the armhole with two holes and buttons and at the opposite hip front by a buttonholed pointed flap. The top edge of the riband should be fashioned to avoid sagging and undue covering of the shirt front.

    Only one riband is worn.

    (ii) Stars are worn on the left breast of the coat. When two stars are worn that of the senior order is placed directly above the other. Three stars are worn in triangular formation, and four stars are worn in a diamond formation. The star of the senior order is worn on top, except that in the case of three stars it is permissible for the two senior stars to be worn in line on top with the junior star beneath. Not more than four stars are worn at any one time.

(b) The insignia of the 2nd Class (Knight Commander) are worn as follows :—

    (i) The neck badge (full size) is worn round the neck as directed in para. 70 (b).

    (ii) Stars are worn on the left breast. The instructions in para. (a) (ii) above also apply to the stars of Knight Commanders.

(c) The insignia of the 3rd Class (Companion or Commander) are ribands and badges worn round the neck. These are worn in the same manner as the ribands and badges of Knight Commanders (see para. 64 (b)).

The foregoing does not apply to the badge of a Companion of the Distinghished Service Order, which is worn on the left breast in the order assigned to it.

(d) The badges of the 4th and 5th Classes (officer or member) are worn on the left breast in the position assigned to them.

(e) Miniature decorations and medals are worn on the left lapel of the coat in one horizontal line, one inch below the point of the shoulder suspended from a bar, of which no part is to be seen.

(f) The instructions contained in para. 61, sub-paras. (i) and (iii) regarding the wearing of miniature medals with mess dress will also apply.

(g) For foreign decorations and medals see para. 74.

72. **Order in which orders, decorations and medals should be worn.**—This in no way affects the precedence conferred by the statutes of certain orders upon the members thereof :—

Victoria Cross.
British Orders of Knighthood, etc.

Order of the Garter.
Order of the Thistle.

British Orders of Knighthood, etc.—contd.

Order of St. Patrick.
Order of the Bath.
Order of Merit (immediately after Knights Grand Cross of the Order of the Bath).
Order of the Star of India.
Order of St. Michael and St. George.
Order of the Indian Empire.
Order of the Crown of India.
Royal Victorian Order (Classes I, II and III).
Order of the British Empire (Classes I, II and III).
Order of the Companions of Honour (immediately after Knights and Dames Grand Cross of the Order of the British Empire).
Distinguished Service Order.
Royal Victorian Order (Class IV).
Order of the British Empire (Class IV).
Imperial Service Order.
Royal Victorian Order (Class V).
Order of the British Empire (Class V).

NOTE.—The above applies to those orders of similar grades. When the miniature or riband of a higher grade of a junior order is worn with that of a lower grade of a senior order, the higher grade miniature or riband should come first, e.g., the miniature or riband of a K.C.I.E. will come before a C.B., and a G.C.M.G. before a K.C.B. Not more than four stars of orders and not more than three neck badges may be worn at any one time in full dress uniform.

Baronets' Badge.—(The badge is worn suspended round the neck by the riband in the same manner as the neck badge of an order and takes precedence immediately after the badge of the Order of Merit. The badge is not worn in miniature and the riband is not worn with undress uniform).

Knights Bachelors' Badge.—(The badge to be worn after the star of a Knight Commander of the Order of the British Empire).

Decorations.

Royal Red Cross (Class I).
Distinguished Service Cross.
Military Cross.
Distinguished Flying Cross.
Air Force Cross.
Royal Red Cross (Class II).
Order of British India.
*Indian Order of Merit (Military). } Orders given only in India.
Kaisar-i-Hind Medal.
Order of St. John.
Albert Medal.

---

* The Indian Order of Merit (military and civil) is distinct from the Order of Merit instituted in 1902.

Medals for Gallantry and Distinguished Conduct.

Medal for Distinguished Conduct in the Field.
Conspicuous Gallantry Medal.
Distinguished Service Medal.
Military Medal.
Distinguished Flying Medal.
Air Force Medal.
Indian Distinguished Service Medal.
Constabulary Medal (Ireland).
Board of Trade Medal for Saving Life at Sea.
*Indian Order of Merit (Civil).
Edward Medal.
King's Police Medal.
Medal of the Order of the British Empire (for Gallantry).
Life Saving Medal of the Order of St. John.

* War Medals (in order of date).

Polar Medals.

Arctic Medal, 1815-1855.
Arctic Medal, 1876.
Antarctic Medal, 1901-1903.

Jubilee, Coronation and Durbar Medals.

Queen Victoria's Jubilee Medal, 1887 (Gold, Silver and Bronze).
Queen Victoria's Police Jubilee Medal, 1887.
Queen Victoria's Jubilee Medal, 1897 (Gold, Silver and Bronze).
Queen Victoria's Police Jubilee Medal, 1897.
Queen Victoria's Commemoration Medal, 1900 (Ireland).
King Edward's Coronation Medal.
King Edward's Police Coronation Medal.
King Edward's Durbar Medal (Gold, Silver and Bronze).
King Edward's Police Medal, 1903 (Scotland).
King's Visit Commemoration Medal, 1903 (Ireland).
King George's Coronation Medal.
King George's Police Coronation Medal.
King's Visit Police Commemoration Medal, 1911 (Ireland).
King George's Durbar Medal (Gold,† Silver and Bronze).

---

* Medals awarded for services during the Great War (1914-1919) should be worn in the following order :—1914 Star, 1914-1915 Star, British War Medal, Mercantile Marine War Medal, Victory Medal, Territorial Force War Medal, India General Service Medal (for operations in Afghanistan, 1919).

† King George's Durbar Medal in gold can be worn in the United Kingdom by ruling chiefs India only.

Orders, Decorations and Medals.

Efficiency and Long Service Decorations and Medals.

Long Service and Good Conduct Medal.
Naval Long Service and Good Conduct Medal.
Medal for Meritorious Service.
Indian Long Service and Good Conduct Medal (for Europeans of Indian Army).
Indian Meritorious Service Medal (for Europeans of Indian Army).
Royal Marine Meritorious Service Medal.
Royal Air Force Meritorious Service Medal.
Royal Air Force Long Service and Good Conduct Medal.
Indian Long Service and Good Conduct Medal (for Indian Army).
Indian Meritorious Service Medal (for Indian Army).
Volunteer Officers' Decoration.
Volunteer Long Service Medal.
Volunteer Officers' Decoration (for India and the Colonies).
Volunteer Long Service Medal (for India and the Colonies).
Colonial Auxiliary Forces Officers' Decoration.
Colonial Auxiliary Forces Long Service Medal.
Medal for Good Shooting (Naval).
Militia Long Service Medal.
Imperial Yeomanry Long Service Medal.
Territorial Decoration.
Territorial Efficiency Medal.
Special Reserve Long Service and Good Conduct Medal.
Decoration for Officers of the Royal Naval Reserve.
Decoration for Officers of the Royal Naval Volunteer Reserve.
Royal Naval Reserve Long Service and Good Conduct Medal.
Royal Naval Volunteer Reserve Long Service Medal.
Board of Trade Rocket Apparatus Volunteer Long Service Medal.
Special Constabulary Medal.
Royal Naval Auxiliary Sick Berth Reserve Long Service and Good Conduct Medal.
Royal Fleet Reserve Long Service and Good Conduct Medal.
The King's Medal (for Champion Shots in the Military Forces).
Union of South Africa Commemoration Medal.

Medals belonging to Orders.

Royal Victorian Medal (Gold and Silver).
Imperial Service Medal.
Medal of the Order of the British Empire (awarded prior to 29th December, 1922).

Medals belonging to Orders—contd.

Medal of the Order of the British Empire (for Meritorious Service).
Royal Victorian Medal (Bronze).
Service Medal of the Order of St. John.
Badge of the Order of the League of Mercy.

Foreign Orders (in order of date of award).
Foreign Decorations (in order of date of award).
Foreign Medals (in order of date of award).

The insignia of the Orders of the Garter, the Thistle and St. Patrick are not worn in miniature, neither are ribands to represent them worn in undress and service dress.

The Orders of Merit and of the Companions of Honour are worn in uniform on all occasions except service dress and undress with forage cap. They are also worn in evening dress on all occasions when decorations are worn. These orders are *never* worn in miniature.

73. **Order in which medals granted during the Great War will be worn.**—Stars and medals approved for service during the Great War, also their ribands, will be worn in the following order :—

1914 Star
or
1914-1915 Star.
British War Medal.
Mercantile Marine War Medal.
Victory Medal.
Territorial Force War Medal.
India General Service Medal.
(for operations in Afghanistan, 1919).

74. (*a*) **Foreign orders, decorations and foreign war medals.**—The rules governing the wearing of British orders and decorations also apply to foreign orders and decorations for which full permission has been given.

(*b*) Foreign orders and decorations for which private permission has been given will be worn in full dress, in mess dress, and in evening dress (plain clothes) only on the occasions specified in the letter of authority. The small ribands of such decorations will not be worn in undress or service dress. Miniatures of such decorations will only be worn on the occasions mentioned in the letter of authority when mess dress or evening dress (plain clothes) is worn.

(*c*) Foreign medals, other than war medals, are governed by the same rules as foreign decorations.

A foreign war medal, the wearing of which has been sanctioned by His Majesty, or its riband, or miniature, will be worn in all orders of dress in the same way as British medals.

(*d*) When attending a function organized by, or for the representative of, a foreign state, the order or neck decoration of that foreign state in possession

Orders, Decorations and Medals.

of the wearer should be given precedence over the British order or decoration usually worn. For instance, it would be more appropriate for the holder of a Legion of Honour badge to wear it at an official dinner at the French Embassy in place of the senior badge usually worn.

75. **Wearing of orders, decorations and medals by chaplains of the Royal Army Chaplains Department.**—Orders, decorations and medals will be worn by chaplains of the Royal Army Chaplains Department when on duty at parade services.

ORDERS OF DRESS.

76. The orders of dress are shewn in the following paragraphs.

No. and type of dress.	Articles.	Occasions when worn.	Remarks.
1. Review order. *Service dress (serge or drill).*	Boots, ankle with puttees or leggings or field boots. Breeches or knickerbockers, khaki cord or drill. Gloves if ordered by the G. O. C. District or Independent Brigade. Helmet or lungi, khaki. Frock, khaki, drill. Sword with " Sam Browne." Scabbard and belt (a). Whistle. Spurs, for mounted officers. Orders, decorations and medals, as in para. 62. Revolver (b).	(1) State ceremonies. (2) Royal escorts. (3) Guards on royal residences. (4) Guards of honour. (5) Ceremonies and entertainments when it is considered desirable to do special honour to the occasion. Official and public balls, dinners, luncheons or breakfasts and evening receptions as ordered. (6) King's birthday parades. (7) Church parades. (8) Proclamation parades. (9) Funerals.	(a) A temporary commissioned officer will not wear a sword. (b) For Royal Tank Corps officers when mounted with cars, in lieu of the sword.
2. Marching order.	As in review order. Small ribands of orders, decorations and medals. Compass. Field glasses. Greatcoat, waterproof coat or waterproof sheet (if ordered). Haversack. Pocket book (A. B.—153). Pouch ammunition. Revolver. Water-bottle. *Additional for field service.* First field dressing and identity discs.	(1) Active service. (2) Training. (3) Manœuvres. (4) Marches. (5) Inspections. (6) Annual range courses. (7) As may be specially ordered.	
3. Drill order.	As in review order. Small ribands of orders, decorations and medals.	(1) Divisional and brigade parades as may be ordered. (2) General courts-martial. (3) District courts-martial, station boards, committees and courts of enquiry. (4) Regimental courts-martial and boards. (5) All ordinary parades, riding school and regimental duties and examinations for promotion. (6) As may be specially ordered.	
4. Mess order.	Mess dress as authorised in these regulations with miniature orders, decorations and medals.	(1) Dining at naval, military or air-force messes. (2) At naval, military and air-force evening entertainments and dances. (3) Dining with His Excellency the Viceroy, Governors, the Commander-in-Chief, or when specially invited to meet these officers; with a general officer commanding or flag officer of the navy. (4) Dining on board a Government transport. (5) As may be ordered.	Mess dress will not be worn at manœuvres.

B

The articles of dress mentioned in the above tables do not apply to officers of units for whom equivalent articles of different patterns are laid down in the detailed description of their uniforms (*e.g.*, Highland regiments).

77. In cases where alternative articles of uniform are allowed, all officers of a regiment must be dressed alike.

78. The foregoing orders for dress are applicable to British officers and Indian officers with the King's commission in His Majesty's land forces except that the latter will wear the lungi or pagri instead of the helmet if they so desire. But those who elect to wear the lungi or pagri on parade must also wear it with mess dress. All other Indian officers will comply as far as possible, but in service dress will wear the stand-up collar.

79. **Other ranks.**—For soldiers of the British service the orders are prescribed in the King's Regulations for Indian other ranks the orders therein will conform. Due regard will be paid to the orders in these regulations, and in Clothing Regulations, India.

80. **On board ship.**—Service dress and mess dress will be worn. Departmental officers for whom an outfit allowance is not admissible may, if they so desire, wear evening dress at dinner in lieu of mess dress.

The wearing of uniform by retired officers and officers returning to England on leave pending retirement is optional, but mess dress or evening dress will be worn at dinner.

Officers sailing from India in vessels other than government transports will wear plain clothes while on board.

81. **On active service.**—The articles of uniform required are detailed in the field service manuals of units.

82. **Horse furniture.**—Officers' horse furniture will include the head-rope in all orders of parade. On field service and when specially ordered, mess tins, nose bags, picketing-gear, horse's blanket, grass nets and surcingle pads will be carried.

Branch of service.	Review order.	Marching order.	Drill order.
Staff	Saddle. Bridle complete. Wallets (general officers wear the gold lace flounce over the wallets and the saddle-cloth, except when "staff in blue" is the order of dress). Great-coat when ordered carried behind the saddle. Shoe case.*	As for review order, but without gold lace cover, flounce, and saddle cloth, for general officers. Great-coat rolled behind saddle. Nose bag.	As for marching order, but without great-coat or nose bag.
Cavalry	Saddle. Bridle complete. Wallets. Leopard or lamb skin if worn. Throat plumes. The great-coat to be carried behind the saddle when ordered. Shoe case.*	As for review order, no leopard or lamb skin or throat plume. Great-coat rolled behind saddle. Nose bag.	As for marching order, but without great-coat, or nose bag.
Royal Artillery	As for cavalry	As for cavalry	As for cavalry.
Royal Engineers	As for infantry	As for infantry	As for infantry.
Infantry and Royal Tank Corps.	Saddle. Bridle complete. Wallets. Shoe case.* Throat plumes in units for which they are authorised (Great-coat behind the saddle when ordered).	As for review order but without throat plumes, and with the following additions :— Nose bag. Great-coat rolled behind saddle.	As for marching order, but without great-coat or nose bag.

* In review order the shoe case is worn in "Hot weather khaki" only.

Branch of service.	Review order.	Marching order.	Drill order.
Army Remount Department.	As for cavalry	As for cavalry	As for cavalry.
Indian Army Service Corps. Indian Medical Service. Military Accounts Department.	As for infantry	As for infantry	As for infantry.

Aides-de-camp, aides-de-camp general, equerries, extra equerries, honorary physicians, honorary surgeons and honorary chaplains to the King-Emperor, equerries to the Prince of Wales and other members of the Royal Family.

83. Uniforms and distinctions as described in Dress Regulations for the Army.

The special uniforms and horse furniture laid down in paras. 68 to 99. Dress Regulations for the Army for aides-de-camp to the King, are, with the exception of the aiguillette, abolished.

Aides-de-camp to the King, who are in possession of the uniform and horse furniture formerly prescribed for that appointment, may, however, continue to use it until requiring replacement.

84. Aides-de-camp to the King will wear regimental uniform, substantive colonels and officers holding the honorary rank of brigadier-general or of major-general, the uniform of their rank.

85. The Royal Cypher and crown takes the place of badges of rank on the shoulder cords or shoulder straps of the tunic, and the aiguillette on the right shoulder will be worn with the tunic on all occasions.

86. With mess dress and service dress the Royal Cypher (without a crown) is placed as follows :—

Colonels and brigadiers.—

Immediately below the crown of rank.

Hon. and temporary brigadier generals and hon. and temporary major generals :—

Immediately below the crossed sword and baton.

Major generals, lieutenant generals and generals :—

Immediately above the crossed sword and baton.

87. **Honorary physicians, honorary surgeons, and honorary chaplains to the King.**—Officers holding the appointments of honorary physician, honorary surgeon and honorary chaplain to the King will wear the Royal Cypher.

The device will not be worn when the officers have ceased to hold the appointments.

The Royal Cypher will be worn as follows :—

Honorary physicians and honorary surgeons to the King.—The Royal Cypher and crown will take the place of badges of rank on the shoulder cords or shoulder straps of the full dress tunic. With mess dress, undress and service dress, general officers will wear the Royal Cypher immediately below the crossed swords and baton. In the case of colonels, the Royal Cypher will be placed immediately above the stars and below the crown.

Honorary chaplains to the King.—The Royal Cypher will be worn in mess dress and service dress as described above. This distinction will not be worn when the officers have ceased to hold the appointment.

88. Wearing of the Royal Cypher and crown or the Royal Cypher in miniature by ex-aides-de-camp general and ex-aides-de-camp to the King.

An A. D. C. after vacating the appointment except an officer who vacates the appointment on promotion to the substantive rank of major general, will wear the Royal Cypher in miniature immediately below the crown of rank on the shoulder straps of all uniform garments.

An A. D. C. general, after vacating the appointment will wear the Royal Cypher in miniature immediately above the crossed sword and baton, except hon. brigadier generals and hon. major generals who will wear the Royal Cypher and crown in miniature immediately below the crossed sword and baton.

Officers who vacate the appointment of A. D. C. on promotion to the substantive rank of major general will cease to wear the Royal Cypher.

Ex-A's. D. C. general and ex-A's. D. C. on retirement will wear the Royal Cypher, or the Royal Cypher and crown, as detailed above.

89. Officers of the Indian army who are appointed extra equerries to H. R. H. the Prince of Wales will wear the aiguillette, laid down for equerries in the Dress Regulations for the Army at the viceregal court in India, at all courts elsewhere, and when they meet His Royal Highness.

The special aiguillette worn by Indian orderlies to His Majesty the King-Emperor will be retained by them on their return to India but will only be worn at durbars, and at functions at which His Excellency the Viceroy may be present, on the Sovereign's birthday parade in India, and on the 1st January proclamation parade.

The following is a description of this special aiguillette :—

Wire cord $\frac{1}{4}$ inch gold, with plait and cord loop in front ; and same at back, the plaits ending in plain cord with gilt metal tags. The plaits and cords front and back are joined together by a short gold braid strap in which is worked a button-hole. The aiguillette is attached to the right shoulder of the garment by a button placed under the outer end of the shoulder cord or strap. The long cord is looped up on the top or front cord and the short and long plaits are fastened together, and a small gold braid loop is fixed thereon to attach to the top button of the garment on the side on which the aiguillette is worn. The arm is passed between the front plait and cord and the back or long plait and cord.

Military secretaries and aides-de-camp to the C.-in-Chief, G. Os. C.-in-chief, commands, and G. Os. C., districts.

90. Uniform as described for staff and personal appointments in para. 107, *et seq*. Plume as in para. 91.

Personal appointments* to the Viceroy and Governor General of India.

Full dress.

91. **Badges and devices.**—*On buttons.*—The Garter surmounted by a Tudor Crown, within the Garter, the Royal Cypher. *On tunic.*—The lotus leaf. *On waist plate.*—In silver the Royal Cypher and Tudor Crown encircled with oak leaves, on the bottom of the wreath a scroll inscribed "DIEU ET MON DROIT."

Boots.—Wellington, patent leather.

Cocked hat.—Staff pattern with upright loop of ¾-inch purl lace; tassels netted, gold purl head, 8 small gold bullions, with 7 crimson bullions under them. Plume of red and white upright swan feathers, 5 inches long. (Worn in full dress and with the frock coat when the helmet is not worn.)

Embroidery.—Gold, lotus-leaf device.

Gloves.—White kid.

Helmet.—White, cork, Wolseley pattern, gilt spike.

Lace.—Gold, oak-leaf pattern.

Pagri.—White muslin.

Plume.—Red swan feathers, 7-inches long, drooping outwards, with white feathers under, reaching to the end of the red ones.

Sash waist.—Gold and crimson silk net; plaited runner and fringe tassels of gold and crimson silk.

Scabbard.—Steel, with gilt mountings.

Spurs.—Brass.

Straps.—Blue cloth.

Sword.—Mameluke gilt hilt, with device of the Royal Cypher and Crown; ivory grip, scimitar blade.

Sword belt.—Russian leather, 1½-inches wide, with slings 1-inch wide; three stripes of gold embroidery on belt and slings; a gilt hook to hook up the sword.

Sword knot.—Gold and crimson round cord strap, with gold and crimson acorn.

Trousers.—Blue cloth, with 1¾-inch scarlet cloth stripes down the side seams.

Tunic.—Scarlet cloth, with blue cloth collar and cuffs, the skirt 12 inches deep for an officer 5 feet 9-inches in height. On each side in front 8 embroidered loops with device of lotus leaves, 5 of them with buttons above

---

* Except private secretary who, if a military officer, wears his military un'form.

the waist, and 3 without buttons below it. A similar loop on each side of the collar. Round cuffs. 3-inches deep. A scarlet flap on each sleeve, with 3 embroidered loops and large buttons, each loop 1¾ inches long exclusive of the drop. A scarlet flap on each back skirt, 10 inches long and 2 inches wide, with 2 loops and buttons similar to those on the sleeve ; 2 buttons at the waist behind. A gold aiguillette. the cord $\frac{13}{40}$ inch in thickness, on the right shoulder, and a gold cord twisted loop, with a small button on the left. The collar cuffs, flaps, and back skirts edged with white cloth, ¼-inch wide, and the skirts lined with white. Hooks and eyes in front. No shoulder-straps or badges of rank.

Scarlet undress.

92. **Tunic.**—The same as the dress tunic, except that there are straight single line loops of scarlet mohair cord, instead of gold embroidery, and on the collar a straight single blue cord loop with a small button at each end exacted over the button of the shoulder cord ; small buttons on the cuffs.

All other articles as in full dress.

For mounted duties (scarlet undress).

93. **Boots.**—Butcher.

Pantaloons.—Blue cloth, with 1⅔-inch scarlet cloth stripes down the side seams.

Spurs.—Brass, swan neck, brass foot chains and patent leather spur straps.

Blue undress.

94. **Boots.**—Wellington, patent leather.

Forage Cap.—Staff pattern, band of scarlet cloth.

Frock Coat.—Blue cloth, single breasted, to button down the front with eight holes and buttons, eight single line loops of blue silk twist on each side of the breast ; a similar loop on each side of the collar, with a small button at the end of each exactly over the button of the shoulder cord. Plain cuffs with four holes and buttons to each. A flap on each skirt behind, with a button at the bottom. A gold (gimp cord undress) aiguillette, the cord ¼ of an inch in thickness on the right shoulder, and a gold (gimp twisted) cord with a small button on the left ; two buttons at the waist behind. The skirts lined with black. A pocket inside each skirt behind. No badges of rank.

Blue serge frock (jumper).—Blue serge with staff gorget patches as described in Part I, General Instructions and staff buttons.

Straps.—Blue cloth.

Sword, scabbard, sword belt, sword knot, sash spurs.—As in full dress.

Overalls.—Blue cloth, with scarlet stripes 1¾-inches wide down the side seams.

For mounted duties (blue undress).

95. **Frock coat or blue serge frock (jumper).**—As ordered.

Pantaloons, boots, spurs.—As in scarlet undress.

Evening undress (mess dress).

96. **Dress coat.**—Blue cloth, black velvet collar. Breast faced with "Star of India" blue silk, skirts lined with same ; 3 buttons, gilt, mounted, the Royal Cypher and Imperial Crown, on each front, 2 at waist behind and 4 smaller buttons on each sleeve.

Waistcoat.—White, single breasted, 3 gilt buttons.

Trousers.—Black, plain.

Hot weather uniform.

97. A plain white patrol jacket with breast pockets, gilt buttons, with braiding on the sleeves only, plain collar with white linen collar inside to show $\frac{1}{8}$ inch. Gold full or undress aiguillette on right shoulder as the case may be with gold twisted cord on left, plain white overalls, black leather straps. Gloves will not be worn.

Horse furniture.

98. **Bridle.**—Universal pattern, with dark blue enamel brow band and rosettes.

Saddle.—Universal pattern.

Saddle cloth.—Blue cloth, lined moleskin, laced, all round with one inch gold lace ; at each hind corner a "Star of India" badge (silver star), with gilt motto, and gold embroidery outside.

General instructions.

99. **Blue undress (frock coat).**—Will be worn at reviews and inspection when H. E. the Viceroy is present, on ordinary occasions by the A.-D.-C. in waiting and at receptions of, and visits to, Indian chiefs, where 'undress' is stated in the programme.

Blue serge frock (jumper).—Will be worn by the aide-de-camp in waiting when on ordinary duty in the house and by the staff when the Viceroy attends manœuvres or field days mounted. Swords will not be worn with the "jumper".

Cocked hat.—Will be worn with full dress or frock coat, when the helmet is not worn.

Evening undress (mess dress).—Will be worn when dining at Government House, or at other houses, when in attendance on, or to meet the Viceroy ; also at the house of the C.-in-C., and of the governor of a presidency or province within his government.

Forage cap.—Will be worn with the jumper.

Full dress.—Will be worn at levees. drawing-rooms, and all evening entertainments where the staff appear in uniform, and on such state occasions as shall be specially ordered.

Gloves.—Will be worn on all occasions, except with the jumper.

Helmets.—Will be worn on all outdoor duties as may be ordered. Plume will be worn with the helmet in full dress, gilt spike in undress.

Honorary aides-de-camp.—When in attendance on the Viceroy, will wear their ordinary uniform with a gold aiguillette, the cord ¼ inch in thickness, on the right shoulder over their tunics, blue frock coats, or patrol jackets. In the case of the officers of the Auxiliary Force, India, a silver aiguillette will be worn.

Honorary surgeons.—On state occasions only, will wear in uniform a full dress aiguillette, on the right shoulder, instead of a gold sash.

Scarlet undress.—Will be worn on all mounted full dress duties.

Indian aides-de-camp to His Excellency the Viceroy.

(Except Gurkha officers who wear the same uniform as British officers of their regiments but with aiguillette.)

Full dress.

100. **Aiguillette, sword belt and knot.**—As in para. 91.

Boots.—Hessian.

Gloves.—White doeskin.

Kamarband.—Blue kashmir, with gold embroidered work.

Frock coat.—Scarlet serge, to reach to knee. Body lined with scarlet italian and sleeves with striped silesia. Open behind from waist to the bottom of skirt, the left skirt passing over the right by about $1\frac{3}{4}$-inches. Collar of blue cloth lined with black italian $1\frac{1}{4}$-inches deep, square in front and fastened with 2 hooks and eyes. Along the top and ends of the collar there is a row of lace (padded) with a row of gold braid eyes inside the lace. Cuffs pointed of blue cloth, $4\frac{3}{4}$-and $2\frac{1}{4}$ inches deep at the front and sides respectively. Along the top of the cuff there is a row of lace (padded on the top half of the sleeve only) the point extending to $6\frac{1}{2}$-inches from the bottom of the cuff. Above the lace there is a row of gold braid eyes extending to $8\frac{1}{2}$ inches from the bottom of the cuff—below the lace there is a similar row of gold braid eyes except that front where it is formed into a figurette ; the latter reaches to the bottom of the cuff. A twisted loop on left shoulder, the right shoulder plain for aiguillette. Five large buttons down the front, the top one $1\frac{1}{2}$-inches from bottom of collar, the lowest 3-inches from waist seam. Two buttons on the waist seam behind, and a small one on the left shoulder for twisted loop. On the waist seam of the left forepart there is a brass hook fastened to a loop of scarlet silk on the right side. There is a similar hook at the extreme point of the right skirt, in front, fastened to a loop of scarlet silk on the inside of the left skirt 3-inches from the front to prevent the right skirt from drooping in front.

Lace.—Gold, oak-leaf, $\frac{3}{4}$ inch.

Lungi.—Blue with gold edging.

Pantaloons.—White cloth reaching to within 5-inches from the ground, opening at the bottom of the side seam for 7-inches, fastened with three small pearl buttons. White bone brace and fly buttons at the top. Large strappings of body cloth reaching to within $10\frac{1}{2}$-inches from the top and 8 inches from the bottom of the pantaloons. Two cross pockets.

Pouch.—The flap is pointed, and made of leather covered with blue cloth, and lined with red morocco leather, 7-inches long and 5¼-inches broad at the bottom, gradually widening to 6-inches broad at the top. The edge of the flap is braided with lace gold ½-inch, oak-leaf pattern. A badge, gold embroidered Royal and Imperial Cypher with crown above, and the motto " DIEU ET MON DROIT " on two scrolls underneath on the front of the flap. The pocket is of tin 2-inches deep and 5¼-inches broad and covered with red morocco leather, a brass stud at the bottom for fixing flap. The pouch is attached to the belt by gilt metal dees with swivels.

Pouch belt.—Of red morocco leather 2⅝ inches wide, of the length required, tapering off to a tab 3-inches long at each end with button hole 1 inch from end of each tab, which is fastened back to a brass stud 4¼-inches from the end of each tab. The outside of the belt is covered with gold lace, oak-leaf pattern, 2½-inches wide, the ends of the lace finished off at the end of each button hole.

Scabbard.—Steel.
Sword.—As in para. 91 for personal appointments.
Spurs.—Brass, jack, with foot chains.

Blue undress.

101. **Aiguillette.**—As in para. 94.

Frock coat.—Blue serge, similar to full dress except that black mohair lace and braid is used instead of gold, and the body is lined with black italian.

Kamarband.—Red kashmir.

Other articles as in full dress.

Hot weather uniform.

102. **Frock coat.**—White drill reaching to the knee. opening at the back skirt of 18-inches. Plain stand-up collar 1¼-inches in depth, square at front and fastened with two hooks and eyes.

Cuff formed with lace, white, 1⅛-inches. The point of the lace 5-inches from bottom of cuff. The lace is traced on both sides with white braid forming an austrian knot above and below. Five large buttons down the front.

On the waist seam of the right forepart there is a metal button which fastens to a small tab on the left side. One hook at the extreme point of the right skirt which fastens to an eye 3-inches from the front of the left skirt.

Pyjamas.—White cotton, Jodhpur pattern, with a draw of string of white cotton tape.

Socks.—White cotton silk finish.

Shoes.—Balmoral patent leather.

Personal appointments to Governors of provinces.

103. **Uniform.**—As described for staff and personal appointments in paragraph 107, *et seq.*

Plume.—As in paragraph 91.

Aiguillette.—Is worn on the right shoulder.

Evening undress.

104. Dress coat.—Blue cloth ; velvet collar ; breast faced with silk colour as shewn in paragraph 98 ; four gilt buttons on each breast (three in the case of Assam) four on each sleeve and two behind. In Assam the tails are lined with the same colour silk as is used for the breast facings.

Waistcoat.—White, with three gilt buttons (four in the case of Central Provinces).

Trousers.—Black plain. In the Central Provinces the trousers are striped with a double row of black braid.

105. Colour of facings.—Used on the dress coat.

Madras	} Yellow.
United Provinces	
Bombay	
Punjab	
Central Provinces	} Primrose yellow.
Bihar and Orissa	
Burma	
Bengal	} Pale primrose yellow.
Assam	

General instructions.

106. Evening undress.—Will be worn when dining at Government House or at other houses, in attendance on, or to meet the governor or G. Os. C.-in-chief, commands. Also at the houses of a governor of a presidency or province, and of a G. O. C.-in-chief command within his government or command. It will not be worn at private parties when the governor is not present or at regimental messes or when on leave.

Frock.—The frock may be worn by the A.-D.-C. in waiting within the precincts of Government House, and on parades when the officers of the army or divisional staff, appear in that dress.

Full Dress.—Will be worn at state reviews, levees, durbars, drawing-rooms, state occasions, when escorting Indian chiefs, and at evening entertainments when so ordered.

Helmets.—Will be worn on all duties out of doors during the day.

White uniform.—The white frock with white trousers may be worn by the A.-D.-C. in waiting, during the hot weather.

Horse furniture.—Horse furniture will be used on all mounted duties when belts and swords are worn.

STAFF AND PERSONAL APPOINTMENTS.

Officers of the headquarter, general and administrative staffs and officers holding personal appointments, not belonging to a corps or department.

107. The uniform and horse furniture of their rank with the following additions :—

Aiguillette.—Worn on the left shoulder with the tunic and frock coat. Cord ¼ inch gold and red orris basket, with plait and cord loop in front and at back, the plaits ending in plain cord with gilt metal tags. The plaits and cords, front and back, are joined together by a short scarlet cloth strap, in which is worked a button hole. The aiguillette is attached to the shoulder of the tunic or frock coat by a button placed under the outer end of the shoulder cord. The long cord is looped up on the top of front cord, the front cord and the short and long plaits are fastened together, and a small gold braid loop is fixed thereon to attach to the top button of the tunic or the lower hook of the collar of the frock coat. When the O.M., C.V.O., or any neck decoration is worn with the frock coat, the aiguillette will be fixed to the top button on the side on which it is worn. The arm is passed between the front plait and cord and the back or long plait and cord.

Aides-de-camp to the King Emperor wear their special aiguillettes on the right shoulder.

108. **Forage cap and badge.**—General officers, universal pattern, blue cloth scarlet band and welts blue welt round crown, peak as in para. 26. Badge, in gold embroidery on blue cloth the Royal Crest with crossed sword and baton within a laurel wreath, blade of the sword in silver. Other officers, universal pattern, blue cloth with scarlet band and welts, blue welt round crown. Peak as described in para. 26 ; badge, the royal crest in gold embroidery on blue cloth.

109. **Gorget patches.**—As described in para. 34.

110. **Service dress.**—Jacket. as in para. 39 with helmet, and breeches, footwear as authorised (see paras. 38, 20, 22 and 18).

Officers of the headquarter, general and administrative staffs, and officers holding personal appointments, belonging to a corps or department.

111. **Full dress.**—Full dress of unit, aiguillette as described in para. 107 on the left shoulder. Aides-de-camp to the King-Emperor and officers of the household cavalry wear their special aiguillettes on the right shoulder. White Wolseley helmet with plume and chain, staff officers belonging to regiments dressed in drab wearing the drab helmet will wear their regimental helmet with spike and chain.

Forage cap and badge.—As in para. 108.

Great-coat.—Universal pattern as described in para. 35.

Horse furniture.—Universal pattern. Brow band and rosettes, regimental.

Mess dress.—Regimental.

112. **Review order, staff in blue.**
White Wolseley helmet, with gilt metal spike and chain.
Frock coat.—Universal pattern as described in para. 30 staff aiguilltte. Buttons regimental. Officers of rifle regiments and regiments dressed in green and drab wear gilt burnished buttons with the Garter and motto surmounted by a crown; within the Garter the Royal Cypher.
Pantaloons and trousers.—Blue cloth, with scarlet stripes $1\frac{3}{4}$-inches wide.
Sword, belt, girdle, waistsash dirk-belt and slings.—Regimental pattern. Officers of rifle regiments and regiments dressed in green and drab wear a belt of russian leather, $1\frac{1}{2}$-inches wide, gold laced, staff pattern, with gold laced slings 1-inch wide, and lion head buckles. Waist plate, rectangular gilt burnished plate, bearing in silver, the Royal Cypher surmounted by a crown, an oak branch on each side, and a scroll inscribed "DIEU ET MON DROIT" below. Officers of Highland regiments wear the claymore attached by gold laced slings to the dees of the dirk-belt.

Staff officers of the Indian army, below the rank of general officer, may wear their regimental serge frocks with other articles of their full dress regimental uniform as review order, staff in blue. The aiguillette and pouch belt are not worn with the serge frock.

113. **Service dress.**—Regimental. Footwear as in para. 18.

Officers of the headquarters staff, and officers of the general administrative and personal staff.

114. **Service dress.**—Regimental.

115. **Mess dress.**—As in para. 121 for officers of the rank of substantive colonel and above; other officers, regimental.

116. **Staff distinctions.**—The aiguillette is worn with tunic and frock-coat, armlets (para. 12) are worn with service dress by officers of the following formations as described below :—

Armlets.

Formation.	Armlets.		Distinguishing letters.	
	Colour of armlet.	Colour of lettering.	Branch of Staff or Directorate.	Lettering.
Staff of H. E. the Viceroy	Light blue cloth with Imperial Cypher and crown above, embroidered in gold.	..	....	No lettering.
Army Headquarters	French grey cloth with royal crest in metal.	Black below crest.	(*i*) Army secretariat	A. D.
			(*ii*) Military Secretary's staff	M. S.
			(*iii*) Aides-de-Camp	A. D. C.
			(*iv*) General Staff	G.

Staff and personal appointments.

Armlets—contd.

Formation.	ARMLETS.		DISTINGUISHING LETTERS.	
	Colour of armlet.	Colour of lettering.	Branch of Staff or Directorate.	Lettering.
			(v) Adjutant-General's staff	A.
			(vi) Quartermaster General's staff.	Q.
			(vii) Master General of the Ordnance staff.	M. G. O.
			(viii) Royal Artillery	A gun in worsted embroidery.
			(ix) Royal Engineers	R. E.
			(x) Supply and Transport services.	S. T.
			(xi) Medical services, including Director-General. Indian Medical Service Officers.	M.
			(xii) Ordnance services	O.
			(xiii) Veterinary services	V.
			(xiv) Remount services	R.
			(xv) Judge Advocate General's officers.	J.
			(xvi) Signal service	S.
			(xvii) Auxilary and Territorial Force officers.	A. T. F.
(2) Command Headquarters.	Red, black and red	Scarlet	As in the respective cases at Army Headquarters, but officers below major-general's rank holding combined A. and Q. appointments will wear the letters A. and G. on the armlet.	
			Educational officers	A. E. C.
(3) 1st and 2nd Class Districts.	Red	Black	As at command headquarters	
			Staff Captain	S. C.
(4) Brigade Headquarters	Blue	Red	Brigade Major	B. M.
			Staff Captain	S. C.
		Other officers	As at Command Headquarters.	
(5) Station Staff Officer	Green	Black	....	S. S. O.
(6) Other appointments.—				
Assistant Provost Marshal.	Black	Red	....	A. P. M.
Embarkation.—				
Assistant-staff officer	White	Black	....	E. O.
Commandant	White	Black	....	E. C.
Medical section	White	Black	....	E. O. / M.
Supply section	White	Black	....	E. O. / S.
Rest camp	White	Black	....	C A M P
Military attaches	A. H. Q. armlet	Black	....	M. A.

Armlets—*concld.*

Formation.	ARMLETS.		DISTINGUISHING LETTER.	
	Colour of armlet.	Colour of lettering.	Branch of Staff or Directorate.	Lettering.
Military missions (a)	A. H. Q. armlet	Black	....	M. M.
Officers under instruction.	White	No lettering	....	..
Provost Marshal	Black	Red	....	P. M.
Railway Transport Officer.	White	Black	....	R. T. O.
Recruiting officer	Green	Black	....	R. O.
Rest Camps :—				
Bombay and Karachi	White	Black	....	CAMP.
Schools :—				
Small Arms—India	Green, yellow, green.	No lettering	Commandant	..
Small Arms—Pachmari.	Green, yellow, green.	Black	Brigade Major	B. M.
Signal service	Blue and white	Black	....	S.
Staff college	Green, yellow, green.	Black	G. S. duties A. & Q. duties	G. A. Q.
Staff officer to M. G. cavalry.	French grey	Black	....	S. O. M. G. C.
Survey :—				
Companies R. E. (b)	} Blue and yellow	No lettering	....	
Directorates, R. E. (b)				
Sections, R. A. (b)				

(*a*) For officers holding staff appointments when specially ordered.
(*b*) Worn on active service, when performing special duties with other troops at training, manœuvres, etc., or when specially ordered.

GENERAL LIST, INDIAN ARMY.

Field Marshals, general officers, brigadiers and substantive colonels not belonging to a unit, corps or department.

117. Uniform and horse furniture as described in Dress Regulations for the Army.

118. Substantive colonels in command of units wear the uniform of their regiment. Brevet colonels wear the uniform of their substantive rank.

119. **Service dress.**—As laid down in these regulations.

120. **Forage cap.**—Universal pattern. blue cloth with scarlet band and welts. blue welt round crown. Peak as in para. 26. Cover as in para. 28.

121. **Mess dress.**—

Jacket.—Scarlet cloth with blue cloth roll collar, pointed cuffs of blue cloth 6-inches deep at the points, and 2¾-inches behind, a 1-inch slit at the seams. Shoulder straps of blue cloth edged with ½-inch oak leaf pattern (staff pattern for brigadiers and substantive colonels) gold lace, fastened at the points with small mounted buttons. Badges of rank in silver embroidery. No buttons on the front of the jacket and no gold braid or piping.

Vest.—Blue cloth, no collar, fastened with four $\frac{1}{2}$-inch mounted buttons. An open white washing vest without lapels and fastened with four flat gilt buttons may be worn in lieu.

Overalls.—Blue cloth with scarlet cloth stripes. For general officers the stripes are $2\frac{1}{2}$-inches wide and welted at the edges down the side seams. For brigadiers and substantive colonels the stripes are $1\frac{3}{4}$-inches wide down the side seams.

Boots.—Wellington, with box spurs.

Officers of the Indian army not on the cadre of a unit, below the rank of substantive colonel ; officers of the unattached list awaiting admission into the Indian army ; officers of the army in India reserve of officers not posted to a unit, corps or department.

122. **Service dress.**—As laid down in these regulations.

123. **Forage cap.**—Universal pattern (para. 26) blue cloth with band of black oakleaf lace and scarlet welt around the crown. Peak as in para. 26. Covers as in para. 28.

INDIAN ARMY.

124. **Mess dress.—**

Jacket.—Scarlet cloth, with blue cloth roll collar and cuffs. Pointed cuffs, 6-inches deep at the points and $2\frac{3}{4}$-inches behind. Shoulder straps of blue cloth, $1\frac{1}{2}$-inches wide at the base tapering to about 1-inch at the points rounded points fastened with a small button and sewn in at the shoulder. Badges of rank in metal. No collar badges, piping, gold braid or embroidery. No buttons or button holes down the front.

Vest.—White washing, open in front ; no collar ; fastened with four " vest " buttons.

Overalls.—Blue cloth with scarlet welt $\frac{1}{4}$-inch wide down the side seams.

Boots.—Wellington. Mounted officers wear box spurs.

125. **Blank.**

126. **Badges.**—

Rank or department.	On buttons.	On collar of tunic and mess jacket.	On collar of service dress.	On head dress.	On cap.
Field Marshals	Gilt, crossed batons and crown within a laurel wreath.	Nil	Gorget patch (para. 30).	Nil	In gold embroidery on blue cloth, the Royal Crest above crossed batons, within a laurel wreath.
General officers	Gilt, crossed sword and baton within a laurel wreath.	Nil	Gorget patch (para. 30).	Nil	In gold embroidery on blue cloth, the Royal Crest with crossed sword and baton within a laurel wreath, the blade of the sword in silver.

Rank or department.	On buttons.	On collar of tunic and mess jacket.	On collar of service dress.	On head dress.	On cap.
Brigadiers . . . Substantive colonels .	Gilt, burnished. The Garter and motto surmounted by a crown within the Garter the Royal Cypher.	Nil	Gorget patch (para. 30).	Nil	In gold embroidery on blue cloth the Royal Crest.
Officers of the Indian army not on the cadre of a unit, other than those specified above. Officers of the Judge Advocate General's Department; Military Accounts Department; Military Farms Department (see para. 182) other than departmental officers (see para. 183); other than those specified above.	The Royal and Imperial Cypher within a circle inscribed "Indian Army," surmounted by a crown.	Nil	Nil	Nil	As on buttons, the whole encircled by a laurel wreath.
Officers of the unattached list awaiting admission to the Indian army.	Gilt, burnished, with a crown within a scalloped edging.	Nil	Nil	Nil	In gilding metal the Royal and Imperial Cypher surmounted by a crown.
Officers of the Army in India Reserve of Officers not posted to a unit.	Gilt, burnished with a crown within a scalloped edging.	Nil	Nil	Nil	The Royal Cypher and crown embroidered in gold.

British army.

127. Officers on the Indian establishment will conform in details of their dress to such special orders as may be applied to their uniform in India, and deviations from Dress Regulations for the Army which are not in accordance with such orders are not to be permitted.

The orders of dress in these regulations are applicable to all officers.

VICEROY'S BODYGUARD.

British officers.

Full dress.

128. **Badges and devices.**—

On buttons.—The Garter surmounted by a Tudor crown; within the Garter the Royal Cypher.

On tunic.—The lotus leaf.

On waistplate.— In silver the Royal Cypher and Tudor crown encircled with oak leaves; on the bottom of the wreath a scroll inscribed " DIEU ET MON DROIT ".

Boots.—*Mounted.*—Napoleon, patent leather.

Dismounted.—Wellington, patent leather.

Cloak and cape.—Blue cloth to reach the ankles when worn on foot, scarlet shalloon lining gilt ; buttons of regimental pattern ; shoulder straps of the same material as the cloak with small button at the top. Badges of rank in gold on the shoulder-straps.

Embroidery.—Gold lotus-leaf device.

Gauntlets.—White leather.

Girdle.—Gold lace, 2½-inches wide, with 2 crimson stripes, on scarlet morocco leather.

Helmet.—White, cork, Wolseley pattern, with spike of bright gilt metal of regimental pattern, gilt base, leaf pattern.

Lace.—Gold oak-leaf pattern.

Pagri.—White muslin.

Pantaloons.—White, melton cloth.

Pouch.—Gold embroidery and gold braid on blue cloth, and blue morocco leather gilt ends and buttons.

Pouch belt.—Gold oak-leaf lace on scarlet morocco leather, gilt buckle tips, side prickers and chains.

Sabretache.—Gold embroidery and gold oak-leaf lace on scarlet cloth, and scarlet morocco leather, gilt rings and buckles and gold oak-leaf lace slings.

Scabbard.—Steel.

Spurs.—*Mounted.*—Silver plated, swan neck, to buckle with strap and foot chains.

Dismounted.—Brass, box.

Sword.—Cavalry pattern.

Sword belt.—White web with sword suspender and gold lace slings and gilt buckles.

Sword knot.—Gold round cord with gold acorn.

Trousers.—Blue cloth, with one and three-quarter inch lace down the side seams. Black leather foot straps.

Tunic.—Scarlet cloth, with blue collar and cuffs ; the skirt 12-inches deep for an officer 5 feet 9-inches in height. On each side in front 8 straight loops of scarlet mohair cord, 5 of them with buttons above the waist and 3 below it. Embroidered loops with device of lotus leaves on the collar. Round cuffs 3-inches deep. A scarlet flap on each sleeve with 3 buttons. A scarlet flap on each back skirt, 10-inches long and 2-inches wide, with 2 buttons similar to those on the sleeve ; 2 buttons at the waist behind. A gold aiguillette, the cord ¼-inch in thickness on the right shoulder and a gold chain gimp plaited shoulder strap lined with scarlet, on the left shoulder. Badges of rank in silver embroidery on the left shoulder-strap. The collar, cuffs, flaps and back skirts edged with white cloth ¼-inch wide, and the skirt lined with white. Hooks and eyes in front.

Tunic, riding.—The same as the full dress tunic, except that on the collar there are straight single line loops of scarlet mohair cord with a small button at each end exactly over the button of the shoulder strap.

Undress blue.

129. **Aiguillette.**—The same pattern as the undress aiguillette for personal appointments—para. 87.

Boots.—*Mounted.*—Butcher.

Dismounted.—Wellington, plain black leather.

Forage cap.—Blue, gold oak-leaf lace with lancer quarterings. Worn only with the frock coat. In other orders of dress the cap for personal appointments is worn—para. 87.

Frock coat.—Blue cloth, trimmed with black braid, regimental pattern; a shoulder strap of blue cloth on the left shoulder, edged with ½-inch black mohair braid, except at the base, black netted button at top, badges of rank in gold on the left shoulder strap. The undress aiguillette is worn on the right shoulder.

Frock, serge.—Blue, stand-up collar pattern, the collar fastening with two hooks and eyes and having a small stock of the same material at the frock sewn on underneath ; straight single line loops of scarlet mohair cord on the collar, with a small button at each end exactly over the button of the shoulder strap.

Gloves.—White leather with frock coat ; brown with serge frock.

Helmet.—As in full dress.

Pantaloons.—Blue cloth, with scarlet stripes, 1¾-inches wide down the side seams.

Spurs.—As in full dress.

Sword and scabbard and slings.—As in full dress.

Sword belt.—As in full dress.

Sword knot.—As in full dress.

Trousers.—Blue cloth, with scarlet stripes, 1¾-inches wide down the side seams. Black leather foot straps.

Mess dress.

130. **Boots.**—Wellington, patent leather.

Jacket.—Scarlet cloth of regimental pattern, with blue cloth collar and cuffs trimmed with gold lace, shoulder-straps and badges of rank as for tunic.

Waistcoat.—Blue cloth of regimental pattern, trimmed with gold lace.

Spurs.—Brass, box, regimental pattern.

Trousers.—As in full dress.

Hot weather uniform—white.

131. Pre-war pattern : but the frock has blue piping round the bottom of the collar, on the cuffs, up the back sleeve and body seams. Shoulder titles

are not worn. In full dress the aiguillette as for the tunic and in undress as for the frock coat is worn. In drill order neither aiguillette is worn.

The white mess jacket is piped as above and has a stand-up collar fastened with 3 hooks and eyes. White linen collar and black tie are not worn. The kamarband is blue silk.

Horse furniture.

132. **Bridle.**—Universal pattern.

Chain reins.—Steel.

Girths.—Dark blue.

Leopard skin.—Gold fringed and scarlet edging.

Saddle.—Universal pattern.

Shabraque.—Blue cloth, with gold oak-leaf lace and gold embroidery regimental pattern.

Throat ornament.—Red.

Indian officers.

133. **Aiguillette.**—In full dress the same as the full dress of His Excellency the Viceroy's personal appointments, in undress of a similar pattern to that for the personal appointments, but of worsted instead of gold thread.

Boots.—Napoleon, patent leather.

Cloak.—Regulation cavalry pattern, badges of rank in gilt metal.

Frock coat.—Scarlet cloth, fastened with buttons of regimental pattern in front, blue facings and lancer piping ; gold embroidery round neck and in front, regimental pattern ; sleeves, gold lace double lancer pattern raised. Plated shoulder chains, with badges of rank in gilt metal.

Gauntlets.—White leather.

Girdle.—Gold lace, 2½ inches wide, with 2 crimson stripes.

Lungi.—Blue and gold : **Kullah** red and gold.

Pantaloons.—*Full dress*—White cloth.

Undress—Blue cloth.

Pouch and pouch belt.—As for British officers.

Spurs.—Swan-neck with foot chains, silver plated.

Sword and scabbard.—Straight regulation cavalry steel scabbard with rings for full dress and black leather scabbard for undress.

Sword belt.—Gold lace girdle, with gold lace slings.

Sword knot.—Gold line with acorn.

Horse furniture.

134. As for British officers except :—

Shabraque.—Blue cloth, with oak-leaf pattern gold lace edging. No embroidery.

GOVERNOR'S BODYGUARD, MADRAS.

British officers.

Full dress.

135. **Boots.**—*Mounted.*—Butcher.
Dismounted.—Wellington.
Cap lines.—Gold wire.
Cloak.—Regimental pattern.
Gloves.—White leather.
Helmet.—"Wolseley" pattern.
Lace.—Gold, vandyke pattern.
Pagri.—Regimental pattern.
Pantaloons.—White melton cloth.
Pouch belt.—Gold vandyke lace on blue morocco leather, silver buckle, tip slide, prickers and chains.
Pouch box.—Lined blue morocco leather, with silver flap, as for hussars.
Spurs.—*Mounted.*—Silver plated swan-neck, to buckle with strap and foot-chains.
Dismounted.—Gilt box spurs.
Sword and scabbard.—Cavalry pattern.
Sword belt.—Gold vandyke lace on blue morocco leather, gilt buckles, snake fastening.
Sword knot.—Gold line with acorn.
Trousers.—Blue cloth, with double gold vandyke lace stripes.
Tunic.—Scarlet cloth, hussar pattern, with blue cloth collar and cuffs, trimmed as for hussars with gold gimp. Shoulder-cords of plaited gold chain gimp lined with scarlet. Badges of rank in silver embroidery.

Undress.

136. **Forage cap.**—Universal pattern, scarlet, blue band.
Frock coat.—Blue cloth, single-breasted. The collar edged with ¾-inch black braid, and with figuring in narrow braid. A braided figure on each sleeve extending to 10 inches from the bottom of the cuff. Six loops of inch braid across the breast with four rows of olivets. The back seams and back-skirts trimmed with inch braid, traced round with narrow braid, and with olivets and tassels. The skirts lined with black shoulder-straps of the same material as the garment, edged with ½ inch black mohair braid, except at the base; black netted button at the top; badges of rank in gilt or gilding metal.
Pantaloons.—Blue cloth, with double yellow stripes.
Patrol jacket.—Hussar pattern.
Other articles as in full dress. Pouch belt is not worn.

Mess dress.

137. **Mess jacket.**—Scarlet cloth, blue facings, regimental pattern trimmings.

Mess waistcoat.—Blue cloth, trimmed regimental pattern.

Trousers, boots and spurs.—As in full dress.

Hot weather uniform.

138. Pre-war pattern.

Horse furniture.

139. As for hussars.

Shabraque.—Blue cloth, gold embroidery, regimental pattern.

Throat ornament.—Red.

Indian officers.

140. **Alkhalak.**—Scarlet cloth, gold vandyke lace edging $1\frac{1}{2}$ inches wide round neck, breast and cuffs; gold tracing braid round skirts; embroidered sleeves and steel shoulder-chains on blue cloth.

Boots.—Napoleon.

Cloak.—Regimental pattern.

Gloves.—Buckskin.

Horse furniture.—As for British officers.

Kamarband.—Scarlet, of Kashmir work.

Lungi.—Blue and gold.

Pantaloons.—White moleskin.

Spurs.—Swan-neck, silver plated with foot chains.

Sword.—Regimental pattern.

Sword belt.—⎫
             ⎬ Buff.
Sword knot.—⎭

GOVERNOR'S BODYGUARD, BOMBAY.

British officers.

Full dress.

141. **Cap lines.**—Lancer, gold, with acorns.

Cloak.—Regulation cavalry.

Boots.—*Mounted.*—Knee cut with a V at the top.
       Dismounted.—Wellington.

Gauntlets.—White leather.

Girdle.—Gold lace, 2½ inches wide, with 2 blue stripes on blue silk showing at edges.

Horse furniture.—As for hussars.

Kurta.—Scarlet cloth, regimental pattern.

Lungi.—Red, with gold and blue ends.

Lace.—Gold lancer pattern.

Pantaloons.—Blue cloth, with double yellow cloth stripes showing blue light between. White leather for wear with the kurta.

Pouch.—Black patent leather, 6 inches by 2 inches; silver buckles, gilt mountings.

Pouch belt.—Gold lace on blue morocco leather, blue stripe in centre, silver buckles, slide and tip.

Spurs.—*Mounted.*—Jack, crane-necked.

Dismounted.—Box, regimental pattern.

Sword and scabbard.—Cavalry pattern.

Sword belt.—Blue web; slings, gold lace on morocco leather, gilt buckles.

Sword knot.—Gold line with acorn.

Trousers.—Blue cloth, with double yellow cloth stripes.

Tunic.—Scarlet cloth, lancer pattern, trimmed with gold lace, blue lapel, blue piping to back seams of body and sleeves, blue cloth collar and cuffs; shoulder-cords of plaited gold lined with scarlet; badges of rank in silver embroidery.

Undress.

142. **Forage cap.**—Universal pattern, scarlet band.

Frock coat.—Regimental pattern; badges of rank in gilt or gilding metal.

Frock.—Blue serge, regimental pattern.

Gloves.—Brown leather.

Sword belt and knot.—White buff leather.

Other articles as in full dress. Pouch belt is not worn.

Mess dress.

143. Regimental mess dress is worn.

Hot weather uniform.

144. Pre-war pattern.

Indian officers.

145. **Frock coat.**—Scarlet cloth, blue lapel, collar, cuffs and piping. Lacing and shoulder-cords as for British officers' tunic.

Kurta.—Red serge or cloth, facings dark-blue with tracing of gold lace on front and back, regimental pattern.

Lungi.—Red, with gold and blue ends.

Scabbard.—Steel, with a large shoe at the bottom, and a trumpet shaped mouth.

Sword.—Half basket steel hilt, with two fluted bars on the outside black fish skin grip bound with silver wire; slightly curved blade, 35 inches long and $1\frac{1}{4}$ inches wide at the shoulder, grooved and spear-pointed.

Horse furniture.—As for British officers.

Other articles as for British officers.

GOVERNOR'S BODYGUARD, BENGAL.

British officers.

Full dress.

146. **Aiguillette.**—Regulation pattern as worn by all members of the Governor's staff; on right shoulder.

Boots.—*Mounted.*—Butcher.

Dismounted.—Wellington.

Cap lines.—Gold wire.

Cloak.—Bodyguard pattern (para. 128).

Gloves.—White leather.

Helmet.—Wolseley, white, as in para. 38, with brass chain, chin strap and ring behind for attachment of cap lines. Gilt fittings will be worn.

Kurta.—Scarlet, cloth lined to the waist, double breasted, with plastron, collar, and cuffs of sky blue cloth. Cuffs $2\frac{1}{2}"$ at the point, $1\frac{1}{4}"$ at the back seam, with an Austrian knot of hussars' gold chain gimp $8\frac{1}{2}"$ from the bottom of cuff with a line of gold tracing braid on either side. Collar $2\frac{1}{4}"$ high, cut square with a line of $\frac{3}{4}"$ gold universal lace on the outer edge, and a line of hussars' gold chain gimp along the bottom edge of collar. Two rows of plain buttons in front, seven in each row, and one at neck point of plastron. Front fastened with 12 gilt hooks and eyes. Skirts, cut full and to cut the knee when worn dismounted, right skirt cut 5" wider than the fore part, top edge fastened with hook and eye to prevent the fronts gaping when worn dismounted, skirt pleat sewn down, and the centre of back opened from waist seam downwards. Chain patches of body cloth, chains fastened with five gilt hooks and small plain screw button. A small pearl button beneath the right shoulder chain to which the aiguillette is attached.

Lace.—Gold, vandyke pattern.

Lungi.—Dark blue and gold.

Overalls.—Blue cloth with double gold vandyke lace stripes.

Pantaloons.—White melton cloth.

Pouch belt.—Gold vandyke lace on blue morocco leather, silver buckle, tip, slide, pickers and chains.

Pouch box.—Lined blue morocco leather with silver flap.

Spurs.—*Mounted.*—Silver plated hunting to buckle with straps and foot strap.

Dismounted.—Silver plated box spurs.

Sword and scabbard.—Cavalry pattern.

Sword belt.—Gold vandye lace on blue morocco leather, gilt buckles, plate with monogram on buckle fastening.

Sword knot.—Gold line with acorn.

Tunic.—Scarlet cloth, hussar pattern, with sky blue cloth collar and cuffs, trimmed as for hussars with gold gimp. Shoulder cords of plaited gold chain gimp lined with scarlet. Badges of rank in silver embroidery.

Undress.

147. **Forage cap.**—Universal pattern, blue, scarlet band.

Frock coat.—Blue cloth, single breasted. The collar edged with $\frac{3}{4}''$ black braid, and with figuring in narrow braid ; a braided figure on each sleeve extending to 10″ from the bottom of the cuff. Six loops of inch braid across the breast with rows of olivets. The back and back skirts trimmed with inch braid, traced with narrow braid and with olivets and tassels. The skirts lined with black, shoulder straps of the same material as the garment edged with $\frac{1}{2}''$ black mohair braid, except at the base ; black netted button at the top, badges of rank in gilt or gilding metal.

Pantaloons.—Blue cloth with double yellow stripes.

Other articles as in full dress. Pouch belt not worn.

Mess dress.

148. Regimental pattern.

Hot weather uniform.

149. Pre-war pattern.

Horse furniture.

150. As for hussars.

Shabraque.—Blue cloth, gold embroidery, regimental pattern.

Throat ornament.—Red.

Indian officers.

151. **Alkhalik.**—Made of scarlet cloth unlined. Purdah, cuffs and shoulder chain patches of sky blue cloth. $1\frac{1}{2}''$ stand collar of sky blue cloth with gold braid No. 2 bordered $\frac{1}{4}''$ from edge and cut tunic shape at back down to waist, skirts cut full and in two halves, opened at centre of back from waist seam downwards. Fronts cut chapkan pattern the bottom of purdah to be $1\frac{1}{4}''$

above the kamarband. Full length when dismounted to cut the knee cap. Right side of purdah carried through to the bottom of skirt cut large enough to prevent the fronts gaping when worn. A line of lace, gold, 1" with braid, gold No. 2 on either side round fore parts and back of neck showing ⅛" of body cloth between. Top of purdah trimmed in the same manner and piped at neck with body cloth sufficient to show on either side of top tracing. Lace, gold, 1" on top edge of cuff 6" at point and 3" at seams. An austrian knot of cord, gold, universal with braid, gold No. 2 on either side 12" from bottom of cuff, the gold cord, carried up the hind-arm seam of sleeve and down side body seams terminating at waist seam. A small fob pocket on waist seam at right side. The left chain patch sewn completely down to the garment, the right fastened at neck with 2 brass hooks and eyes worked with scarlet silk. The chains fastened by 7 brass hooks one at either point over sleeve head and 4 at top edge of patch. A brass hook in centre of purdah at neck and metal button beneath right chain patch to which the aiguillette is attached. Purdah and fronts fastened with 13 brass hooks and (eyes worked with scarlet silk round purdah only), 4 brass eyes down front to waist seam.

Boots.—Napoleon.

Cape for cloak.—A plain cape made of blue cloth, 3 buttons down front. Buckle and strap on collar. Pocket inside left breast fastened at top with button and button hole. Button hole at centre of collar to fix on cloak. A seam over each shoulder and down centre of back.

Cloak.—Same pattern as worn by the Viceroy's Body Guard. Made of blue cloth, four buttons down front, lined to about 9" from bottom with red serge. One pocket with flap on right side. A gusset inserted at bottom of back to give room over saddle. Pocket in left side seam 7" below scye. Ticket pocket and flap on cuff of left under side sleeve 6½" long. Collar fitted with 3 hooks and eyes, tab underneath to button if required. Button at back to fix belt, sleeves lined with brown linen. Belt (for cloak) made of blue cloth, fitted with a brass buckle on left end and 5 brass eyelet holes on right, 4 feet long with runner of same material to carry loose end of belt.

Gauntlets.—Buckskin.

Kamarband.—Blue, of Kashmir work.

Lungi.—Blue and gold.

Pantaloons.—

White.—White cloth with small knee strappings of same material and machined "V" shaped throughout, 2 cross pockets. Fly vent at bottom of side seam from small downwards fastened with 4 plain buttons.

Blue.—Blue tartan cut to admit of a stripe lace worsted yellow and black to be sewn on top sides. Two cross pockets. Fly vent at bottom of side seam from small downwards fastened with 4 plain buttons. Stays inside to strengthen the knee and leather strappings.

Spurs.—Hunting.

Sword.—Regimental pattern.

Sword belt.—Buff.

Sword knot.—Buff.

Horse furniture.

152. As for British officers except—

Shabraque.—Made of blue cloth edged all round with two rows of 1" gold lace with $\frac{3}{16}$" of scarlet cloth showing on either edge ; monogram B. G. B., gold embroidered, on scarlet cloth, on the back corners.

INDIAN CAVALRY.

153. **Forage cap.**—Universal pattern, para. 26. Other details are shewn in Appendix VIII.

154. **Mess dress.**—

Jacket
Vest } Details are shewn in Appendix VIII.
Overalls

Boots.—Wellington, box spurs.

Badges.—Details are shewn in Appendix IX.

INDIAN INFANTRY AND PIONEER REGIMENTS.

155. **Forage Cap.**—Universal pattern, para. 26. For other details see Appendix X.

156. **Mess dress.**—

Jacket
Vest } Details are shewn in Appendix X.
Overalls

Boots.—Wellington ; mounted officers, box spurs.

Badges.—Details are shewn in Appendix XI.

CORPS, DEPARTMENTS AND MISCELLANEOUS.

157. Officers serving in corps, departments, etc., will continue to wear the uniform of their regiment or corps without addition or alteration until struck off the cadre of their units, when they will wear the dress prescribed for their corps, departments, etc.

Indian Army Service Corps.

158. **Forage cap.**—Universal pattern ; blue cloth with band of blue cloth and white welts.

159. **Mess Dress.**—*Jacket.*—Blue cloth lined with white silk serge, with blue cloth step collar and white cloth facings on the lapel. The facings on lapels cover the lapel only to within $\frac{3}{4}$" of the outer edge, leaving a strip of blue cloth down the outer edge of the lapel.

Plain sleeves with a $3\frac{1}{2}$ inch slit fastened with two small buttons at the hind arm seam.

Shoulder straps of blue cloth 1½ inches wide at the base, tapering to about 1 inch at the points ; rounded points fastened with a small button. The shoulder straps are sewn in at the shoulder.

No buttons or button holes down the front.

Badges of rank in metal.

Collar badges worn on the lapels.

Buttons of corps pattern.

Vest.—White, washing, open in front, no collar, fastened with four vest buttons.

Overalls.—Blue cloth, with two white cloth stripes, ¾-inch wide and ½-inch apart, down the side seams.

Boots.—Wellington ; box spurs.

160. Departmental commissioned officers of the I. A. S. C., will wear the above uniform.

161. Warrant officers of the I. A. S. C., will wear the above uniform with badges of rank in gold embroidery on the right forearm, but the jacket will be of blue serge, No. 1.

162. The provision of mess dress for departmental commissioned officers for whom an outfit allowance is not admissible and for warrant officers is optional.

163. **Badges**—

Department.	On buttons.	On collar of tunic and mess jacket.	On collar of service dress.	On head-dress (helmet, pagri or felt hat).	On cap.
1	2	3	4	5	6
Indian Army Service Corps.	In gilding metal within a circle inscribed "INDIAN ARMY SERVICE CORPS" the Royal and Imperial Cypher. Above the circle a crown.	In silver, on eight pointed star surmounted by a laurel wreath in gold. Within the wreath a white enamel Garter with the motto "HONI SOIT QUI MAL Y PENSE" in gold letters; within the Garter, on a dark blue enamelled back ground, the monogram "I.A.S.C." in gold.	As on forage cap in column (6) but smaller and in bronze and without the black enamelled ground, the monogram pierced.	*Nil.*	On forage cap. In silver, an eight pointed star surmounted by a crown. On the star a laurel wreath. Within the wreath on a black enamelled ground, the Garter and the motto "HONI SOIT QUI MAL Y PENSE," within the Garter the letters "I. A. S. C." in monogram. On service cap.—As in column (4) but larger.

Indian Medical Service.

164. **Forage cap.**—Universal pattern ; blue cloth with band of black velvet.

165. Mess Dress.—*Jacket.*—Blue cloth (Altona), lined with scarlet silk serge, with black corded silk roll collar.

Pointed cuffs of black velvet, 6 inches deep at the points and $2\frac{1}{4}$-inches behind, fastened with three small buttons.

Shoulder straps of blue cloth edged with $\frac{1}{2}$-inch oakleaf pattern gold lace for general officers, and $\frac{1}{2}$-inch staff pattern gold lace for officers of the rank of substantive colonel. $1\frac{1}{2}$ inches wide at the base, tapering to about 1 inch at the points; rounded points fastened with a small button. The shoulder straps are sewn in at the shoulder.

Four small buttons and button holes down the front.

Scarlet cloth edging round bottom of jacket and up to lower end of lapels.

Badges of rank in metal; silver embroidery for general officers and substantive colonels.

Collar badges worn on the lapels.

Buttons of I.M.S. pattern with mounted design.

Vest.—White, washing, open in front, no collar, fastened with four small I.M.S. pattern buttons with mounted design.

Overalls.—Blue cloth, with scarlet stripe, $1\frac{3}{4}$ inches wide, and welted at the edges, down the side seams.

Boots.—Wellington; mounted officers', box spurs.

166. Badges—

Department.	On buttons.	On collar of tunic and mess jacket.	On collar of service dress.	On head-dress (helmet, pagri or felt hat).	On cap.
1	2	3	4	5	6
Indian Medical Service.	On a star a circle surmounted by a crown. The circle inscribed "Indian Medical Service" within the circle the Royal and Imperial Cypher.	Within two laurel branches (gold) a star of eight points (silver) surmounted by a Garter (gold) bearing the motto of the order in letters of gold and enclosing an Esculapius rod in silver, the whole surmounted by an Imperial Crown proper; underneath, on a scroll (silver), the words "Indian Medical Service".	As in column (3), but in bronze.	Nil.	The Royal Crest. (General Officers, in gold embroidery on blue cloth, the Royal Crest with crossed sword and baton within a laurel wreath, the blade of the sword in silver.)

Indian Army Ordnance Corps.

167. Forage cap.—Boat shaped, dark blue cloth, with a narrow gold cord attached to the edges of the crown.

168. Mess Dress.—*Jacket.*—Blue cloth, lined with cotton mercerised white, with scarlet cloth roll collar and cuffs.

Pointed cuffs, 6 inches deep at the points and $2\frac{3}{4}$ inches behind. A 1 inch slit at the seams.

Corps and Departments.

Shoulder straps of blue cloth, 1½ inches wide at the base, tapering to about 1 inch at the points ; rounded points fastened with a small button. The shoulder straps are sewn in at the shoulder.

No buttons or button holes down the front of the jacket and no gold braid or piping.

Badges of rank in metal.

Collar badges in gold embroidery on the lapels.

Vest.—White washing, roll collar, fastened with four vest gilt buttons.

Overalls.—Blue cloth with two scarlet cloth stripes with welted edges, ¾ inch wide and ⅛ inch apart, down the side seams.

Boots.—Wellington ; mounted officers', box spurs.

169. Officers on probation for the I.A.O.C. will continue to wear the mess dress of their regiment or corps without addition or alteration until struck off the cadre of their units when they will wear the mess dress [prescribed for the corps.

170. Departmental ordnance officers of the I.A.O.C. will wear the above uniform.

171. Warrant officers of the I.A.O.C. will wear the above uniform with badges of rank on the right forearm and gilding metal collar badges. The forage cap will be without gold lace and the badge will be the left half of a pair of gilding metal collar badges.

172. The provision of mess dress for departmental ordnance officers for whom an outfit allowance is not admissible, and for warrant officers, is optional.

173. **Badges—**

Department.	On buttons.	On collar of tunic and mess jacket.	On collar of service dress.	On head-dress (helmet, pagri or felt hat).	On cap.
1	2	3	4	5	6
Indian Army Ordnance Corps.	Gilding metal buttons, device as in column (3).	In gilding metal. The Indian Ordnance Arms ; above the shield a crown and below the shield a scroll inscribed " Indian Army Ordnance Corps ". On *collar of mess jacket.* As above but in gold embroidery.	As in column (3). b	As in column (3) but larger for Indian ranks.	As in column (3) for the mess jacket but larger.

Army Remount Department.

174. **Forage cap.**—Universal pattern, blue cloth with yellow band and welts.

175. **Mess Dress.**—*Jacket.*—Blue cloth with yellow cloth roll collar and cuffs.

Pointed cuffs, 6 inches deep at the points and 2¾ inches behind, a 1 inch slit at the seams.

Corps and Departments.

Shoulder straps of blue cloth, 1½ inches wide at the base, tapering to about 1 inch at the points; rounded points fastened with a small button. The shoulder straps are sewn in at the shoulder.

No buttons or button holes down the front of the jacket or on the cuffs, and no gold braid or piping.

Badges of rank in metal; silver embroidery for general officers and substantive colonels.

Collar badges worn on the lapels.

Vest.—Yellow cloth, open in front, no collar, fastened with four vest buttons.

Overalls.—Blue cloth, with two yellow cloth stripes ¾ inch wide and ⅛ inch apart, down the side seams.

Boots.—Wellington; mounted officers', box spurs.

176. Departmental commissioned officers of the A.R.D., will wear the above uniform.

177. Warrant officers of the A.R.D. will wear the above uniform with badges of rank in gold embroidery on the right forearm, but the jacket will be of blue serge, No. 1.

178. The provision of mess dress for departmental commissioned officers for whom an outfit allowance is not admissible, and for warrant officers, is optional.

179. **Badges**—

Department.	On buttons.	On collar of tunic and mess jacket.	On collar of service dress.	On head-dress (helmet, pagri, or felt hat).	On cap.
1	2	3	4	5	6
Army Remount Department.	Plain white metal buttons.	In silver, a horse with a scroll below inscribed "Army Remount Department, India".	As in column (3).	*Nil.*	As in column (3) but larger.

Miscellaneous.

180. Officers of the :—

    (i) Indian army not on the cadre of a unit.

    (ii) Judge Advocate General's Department.

    (iii) Military Accounts Department.

    (iv) Military Farms Department.

    (v) Unattached List awaiting admission into the Indian army will wear the uniform laid down in paragraphs 117 to 124.

181. Blank.

182. **Badges.**—Officers of the Military Farms Department will wear the badges and buttons described below.

Corps and Departments.

Other officers referred to in para. 180 wear the badges and buttons shewn in para. 126.

Department.	On buttons.	On collar of tunic and mess jacket.	On collar of service dress.	On head-dress (helmet, pagri, or felt hat).	On cap.
1	2	3	4	5	6
Military Farms Department.	In brass, the Royal and Imperial Cypher within a circle inscribed "Indian Army" with a crown above.	In silver, the rising sun appearing above a scroll inscribed "Ensem Mutamus Aratro". Resting on the sun the hilts of two crossed swords; a sheaf of wheat in the upper angle of the swords and a sickle in the left and right angles. The end portion of the blades of the sickles passing under the blades of the swords.	In brass, as on collar of tunic and mess jacket.	*Nil.*	As on collar of service dress.

Departmental commissioned and warrant officers of corps, departments, etc., other than those of the Indian Army Service Corps, Indian Army Ordnance Corps, and Army Remount Department.

183. **Forage cap**—Universal pattern, blue cloth without welts with distinctive bands as shewn below :—

> Military Farms—Department.—Grass-green, ⅛-inch light scarlet down the centre.
>
> I.M.D.—Blue cloth with black braid down the centre.
>
> Miscellaneous List and Garrison and Depot Staff.—Blue cloth with scarlet piping on both edges.
>
> Military Engineer Services including Barrack, Public Works, and Sappers and Miners.—Blue cloth with ⅛-inch light scarlet down the centre.
>
> Military Detention Corps.—Scarlet cloth with edging of black mohair tracing all-round.

184. **Mess Dress.**—*Jacket.*—Scarlet serge No. 1 (I.M.D., blue serge, No. 1), lined with drab or scarlet mercerised cotton : roll collar and cuffs of cloth the colour of the facings (see paragraph 186).

Pointed cuffs, 6 inches deep at the points and 2¾ inches behind, a 1-inch slit at the seams.

Shoulder straps of the same material as the jacket, 1½ inches wide at the base tapering to about 1 inch at the points, rounded points fastened with a small button. The shoulder straps are sewn in at the shoulder.

No buttons or button holes down the front of the jacket, or on cuffs, and no gold braid or piping.

Badges of rank in metal.

Collar badges where authorised.

Vest.—White washing, open in front, no collar, fastened with four vest buttons.

Overalls.—Blue cloth, with one 1¾-inch stripe down each side seam (see para. 186).

Boots.—Wellington.

185. The provision of mess dress for departmental commissioned officers for whom an outfit allowance is not admissible, and warrant officers, is optional.

186. *Details of mess jacket, etc.*

| Department. | JACKET. | | | | Overall stripes. |
	Colour.	Collar.	Shoulder straps.	Cuffs.	
Military Farms Department	Scarlet	Grass-green	Scarlet	Grass-green	Grass-green cloth with ¼-inch scarlet right down the centre.
Indian Medical Department	Blue	Black velvet.	Blue	Black velvet.	Scarlet cloth.
Miscellaneous List	} Scarlet	Blue	Scarlet	Blue	Scarlet cloth.
Military Engineer Services, including Barrack, Public Works, and Sappers and Miners.					
Garrison and Depot Staff					
Military Detention Corps	Scarlet	Black	Scarlet	Black	Black mohair lace.

187. Badges—

Department.	On buttons.	On collar of tunic and mess jacket.	On collar of service dress.	On head-dress (helmet, pagri, or felt hat).	On cap.
1	2	3	4	5	6
Departmental commissioned and warrant officers of corps, departments, etc., other than those of the Indian Army Service Corps, Indian Army Ordnance Corps, and Army Remount Department.	The Royal and Imperial Cypher surmounted by a crown with a laurel wreath below.	For the I. D. M., in gilding metal, the Royal and Imperial Cypher surmounted by a crown with a laurel wreath below. The whole standing on a scroll inscribed "Indian Medical Department".	As in column (3).	*Nil.*	In gilding metal, the Royal and Imperial Cypher surmounted by a crown. For the I.M.D., in gold embroidery on blue cloth, the Royal and Imperial Cypher surmounted by a crown with a laurel wreath below.
Indian Corps of Clerks (British Wing).	G. R. I. with laurel wreath and crown.	The Royal and Imperial Cypher.	As in column (3).	*Nil.*	In gilding metal, G. R. I. with laurel wreath and Tudor crown.

188. **Hot weather white mess dress for all units, corps and departments of the Indian Army.**—*Jacket.*—White drill, without braid, or buttons; roll collar, shoulder straps of the same material with a small button at the top;

Corps and Departments.

one inside breast pocket. Sleeves cut plain with pointed cuffs, 5 inches high at point, and 2½ inches behind.

Badges of rank in metal.

Collar badges (where authorised), worn on the lapel.

Units who have been authorised to wear a design of hot weather dress which differs from the details given above are shewn in Appendix XII.

189. *Vest.*—White, washing, open in front, fastened with 4 small buttons. A silk kamarband may be worn in lieu.

190. *Overalls.*—White drill, with black leather footstraps.

191. *Boots.*—Wellington; mounted officers', box spurs.

192. In lieu of the white drill overalls the cloth overalls of the cold weather dress may be worn. All officers of a unit will dress alike.

193. *Kamarbands.*—In lieu of the white waistcoat silk kamarbands may be worn of the following colours, all officers of a unit will dress alike.

Staff	Scarlet.
Indian cavalry—	
Except 3rd Cavalry . .	Colour of facings.
3rd Cavalry	Blue silk, 7 inches wide, with vertical gold and white stripes.
Indian infantry and pioneers	Colour of facings or rifle green for rifle regiments.
Indian Army Service Corps .	Blue.
Army Remount Department .	Yellow.
Military Accounts Department	Blue.
All other corps and departments	Scarlet.

194. **Uniform to be worn by chaplains on field service.**—The uniform particularised below is that authorised to be worn by chaplains of all denominations when on field service. Chaplains in possession of this uniform may also wear it if present on manœuvres, or on the line of march with troops. The wearing of this uniform by chaplains other than chaplains of the Churches of England and Scotland and of the Wesleyan Church will be optional.

Scarf.—Black silk, 7½ inches in width. The monogram " C.F." with the crown above, in gold enbroidery at the ends. The wearing of this scarf by chaplains will be subject to the permission of their own ecclesiastical authority.

Helmet.—Wolseley (para. 38).

Forage cap.—Universal officers, drab service dress pattern with black leather chinstrap and black buttons. Chaplains with relative rank as colonels wear a black cloth forage cap (with drab or khaki cover) with band and welts of purple cloth, and with one row of black oakleaf embroidery on the lower edge of the peak.

Badge for wear on the forage cap in black metal, a cross patée on a plain metal tablet surmounted by a crown.

Jacket.—Serge or drill; universal officers' pattern worn with a white collar and black clerical stock or khaki shirt with soft collar and black tie. Shoulder straps of the same material as the jacket with badges of rank and shoulder title " Chaplain " in black metal.

Gorget patches.—Worn with serge or drill jacket by chaplains with relative rank as colonels only.

Purple cloth with a line of purple silk gimp down the centre and a small gorget button ¾-inch from the point.

Buttons.—Black metal, with device as for cap badge.

Belt.—" Sam Browne " brown leather, without sword frog or sword.

Trousers or breeches.—Service dress pattern.

Putties or leggings.—Service dress pattern.

Boots.—Brown. Ankle or brown field boots may be worn.

Greatcoat or (at option) coat, warm.—Universal officers' pattern. Buttons as for serge jacket.

195. **Officers in civil employ.**—A military officer who is appointed substantively to any civil office for which uniform is prescribed will wear the uniform of that office.

> *Exception.*—Royal Engineer officers and officers of the Indian Medical Service in civil employ who are liable to recall to military duty and are required to maintain their military uniform, are not required to wear civil uniforms, but will wear military uniform on all occasions when military officers wear uniform.

On all State and other occasions when military officers wear uniforms, military officers who are in permanent civil employ, but who do not hold an appointment which carries the right to wear civil uniform, may at their option wear the uniform of the corps or department to which they belonged, or plain clothes.

> *Exception.*—Royal Engineer officers, officers of the Indian Medical Service and Survey of India wear military uniform on all occasions when military officers wear uniform.

Military officers who are temporarily in civil employ will wear their military uniform but may, if they desire, wear plain clothes instead of mess uniform on occasions when the latter is worn by officers in military employ. An officer employed as private secretary to the Viceroy, or a governor will wear military uniform.

The uniform of officers holding political appointments and officers employed with the Imperial Cadet Corps and other corps under the Foreign Department is governed by the orders issued by that department.

The uniform of the officers of the Cantonment Department is governed by the orders issued by the Army Department.

196. **Army in India Reserve of Officers.**—The uniform to be maintained by officers of the A.I.R.O. is given below :—

> *Boots, etc.*—As laid down in para. 18. Black boots and black leggings or coloured putties may be worn by officers serving with regiments which have adopted black boots, etc. (See App. VII.)

Breeches.—Khaki cord or drill laced at the knee, paras. 20-22.

Badges and devices.—As laid down for the unit, corps or department to which posted for duty. If not posted to a unit officers will wear the badges and buttons described in para. 182.

Shoulder titles.—In peace the letters ' A. I. R. O.' will be worn on the shoulder straps below the badges of rank without any other title. On field service the ordinary title of the unit, corps or department to which posted for duty will be worn without the title ' A. I. R. O.'

Cap, forage complete with khaki cover.—As laid down for the unit, corps or department to which posted for duty. If not posted to a unit officers will wear the forage cap prescribed in para. 123.

Greatcoat.—Universal pattern, para. 35.

Helmet.—Universal pattern, para. 38.

Jacket, drill, khaki.—Universal pattern, para. 39.

Putties.—Khaki or coloured as worn by the unit to which posted for duty. (See App. VII).

Sword belt, " Sam Browne ".—Black or brown as worn by the unit to which posted for duty.

Spurs for mounted officers.—As laid down in para 50.

Shirts, khaki.

Khaki soft Oxford collars.—With gold safety pin.

Khaki tie.

Khaki socks.

Trousers, drill, khaki.

The following may be provided voluntarily by officers—

Waterproof coat.—Para. 55.

Service dress (serge).

Mess dress.—(See para. 124.)

197. Retired officers.—Officers who have relinquished their commissions and who have been permitted to retain their rank, or in the case of chaplains who have been appointed honorary chaplains to the forces, also officers who have been demobilized or disembodied, are permitted to wear uniform on special occasions when attending ceremonials and entertainments of a military nature, and on occasions when the wearing of uniform would appear appropriate.

The uniform will be restricted to service dress and mess dress and will be that of the unit or of the general list to which the officer belonged when he relinquished his commission or was demobilized. The badges of rank will be those of the rank he held when demobilized or that retained by him when he quitted the service. The letter " R " will be worn on the collar, below the collar badges where these are worn.

Orders, decorations and medals will be worn with service dress by retired officers on appropriate occasions.

Uniform may not be worn at meetings of a political nature.

198. Queen Alexandra's Military Nursing Service for India—

Winter.—Grey beige or serge ; facings scarlet cashmere.

Summer.—White cambric or drill ; facings scarlet twill cotton.

Belt.—Scarlet cashmere or twill 2-inch deep, fastened hooks and eyes.

Aprons.—(For duty only). White cambric or linen, gored, length to bottom of skirt ; no straps ; one shaped pocket from waist band.

Dresses.—Well cut plain skirt, slightly gathered at back, bodice ; fronts gathered at shoulder into waist band ; 7 scarlet bone buttons down front, regulation size, starting one inch from neck, finishing 1 inch from belt ; plain coat sleeve opening at wrist with 2 scarlet buttons $\frac{1}{2}$ inch and $2\frac{1}{2}$-inch from bottom.

Sisters.—Two 1 inch scarlet bands with an interval of 1 inch —the lower band being 1 inch above the bottom of sleeve.

Senior Nursing Sister.—Plain scarlet cuff 3-inch deep 1 inch from bottom of sleeve.

Lady Superintendents.—Plain scarlet cuff 3-inch deep 1 inch from bottom of sleeve, with scarlet waistcoat.

Chief Lady Superintendent.—Plain scarlet cuff 4-inch deep with 1 inch scarlet band at an interval of $\frac{1}{2}$ inch above ; shoulder strap of scarlet $1\frac{1}{4}$-inch wide at the base tapering to 1 inch at the point with scarlet waistcoat.

Waistcoats.—For lady superintendents only, scarlet cashmere silk or drill 5 inches wide at neck band narrowing down to 2-inch at waist band ; 12 scarlet buttons down front (moulds covered with material).

Caps.—White muslin, handkerchief pattern 1 yard square, plain hem for nursing sisters, hem stitched for lady superintendents and senior nursing sisters.

Cape.—Scarlet cashmere or silk, regulation pattern.

Collars.—Stand up scarlet cashmere or twill, $1\frac{1}{2}$-inch or 2-inch to suit wearer, fastened with hooks and eyes, to be worn with narrow white turn-over collars.

Shoes.—Plain white one strap shoes with rubber heels, with white stockings for white dresses.

Black or grey shoes with rubber heels and grey or black stockings with grey dresses.

Overalls.—White overalls and turn-down white collars may be worn in hot weather. All sisters in the hospital must dress alike.

Coat.—Grey tweed double-breasted, lined scarlet, $\frac{3}{4}$ length, 5 large grey buttons $1\frac{1}{4}$-inch each side suitably spaced, top button being under rever, one pocket with flap each side, top of pocket at level of 2nd button from bottom of coat, $2\frac{1}{2}$-inch turn-down collar, faced with 2-inch scarlet cloth showing $\frac{1}{2}$ inch grey at edge ; 4-inch turn-up grey cuff for sisters and senior nursing sisters.

Lady Superintendents.—Coat as above with the addition of 4-inch cuff with 3 inches scarlet facing.

Chief Lady Superintendent.—Coat as above with the addition of 5-inch cuff with 3-inch scarlet facing and 1 inch scarlet band $\frac{1}{2}$ inch above this.

Corps and Departments. 61

Coat and Skirt.—Grey tweed with scarlet facings for chief lady superintendent, or coat frock.

Helmet.—White Ellwood shape, with white folded pugri, piped scarlet.

Hat.—Optional-plain white black straw panama shape, trimmed 3-inch white silk ribbon with scarlet piping finished on left side with double box-plait. Soft grey felt for winter or field service.

Mess dress.—Same as day dress described above but of white lawn, with scarlet silk facings.

Evening dress.—For official occasions white crepe-de-chine, scarlet silk facings, made exact to uniform design, with the following additions :—

Sister.—One strip of ⅜ inch gold french braid at top edge of first scarlet silk band on sleeve.

Senior Nursing Sister.—One strip of ⅜ inch gold french braid at top edge of 3-inch scarlet silk cuff.

Lady Superintendent.—The same as senior nursing sister with the addition of a strip of ⅜ inch gold french braid round base of collar.

Chief Lady Superintendent.—The same as Lady Superintendent with the addition of one strip of ⅜ inch gold french braid above the 1 inch band on sleeve and shoulder strap.

Buttons.—Both for mess and evening dress, moulds covered scarlet silk same size as bone buttons.

Evening dress.—Optional for nursing sisters.

199. **Nursing Service for Indian Troops' Hospitals.**—*Uniform.*—White ; facings, navy blue twill or cashmere.

Belt.—Navy blue twill, 2 inches wide fastened with hooks and eyes.

Dresses.—*Matrons.*—White cambric or drill, cut in one piece, fronts gathered at shoulder into waist band. 7 navy blue buttons down front, starting one inch from collar and finishing one inch from waist belt : navy blue up-standing collar 1½ inches deep with white muslin turn-over collar to cover not more than one-third of blue collar. Plain coat sleeve to wrist with 3-inch navy blue cuff one inch above button of sleeve. Well cut white skirt slightly gathered at back ; 6-inch hem at foot : length 4 inches above ankle. One patch pocket on either side of front with navy blue piping one inch from top of pocket. Overalls, with navy facings and turn-down white collars may be worn in hot weather.

In cold climates navy blue washing serge or drill may be worn with plain white turn-down collars and cuffs. A white or navy blue knitted sports coat may be worn when the climate necessitates this.

Staff Nurses.—White overalls, turn-down white collars fastened at neck, fronts gathered at shoulder : no yoke. 2-inch box plait down front with 7 navy blue bone buttons two inches apart to start one inch from neck. Navy blue belt to be worn fastened between sixth and seventh button on overall. One patch pocket on either side below belt with narrow navy blue piping one inch from top of pocket. Sleeve plain, elbow length.

Sisters.—Same as above with 1 inch navy blue band 1 inch from bottom of sleeves.

Caps.—White muslin, handkerchief pattern ¾ yard square, hem stitched for matrons, and with one inch plain hem for sisters and staff nurses.

Hats.—Plain white straw, Panama shape, with 1½-inch wide navy blue ribbon, finished left side double box plait.

Helmet.—White, with white folded pugri with narrow navy blue piping.

Shoes.—Plain white one-bar shoes with rubber heels.

Stockings.—White.

Cape.—White, with 2-inch hem, 2-inch navy blue band above hem.

Evening dress.—For wear at official entertainments :—

Matrons.—Dress of white silk with navy blue facings buttons, moulds covered with blue silk same size as bone buttons.

Sisters and Staff Nurses.—Optional.—White cambric. Facings, navy blue silk.

Cape.—White silk for matrons and cambric for sisters and staff nurses, with navy blue silk band in all cases.

APPENDIX I.

BELT AND SWORD KNOT (UNIVERSAL PATTERN).

(a) The "Sam Browne" belt.

(Worn by officers of all branches of the service.)

The belt complete, consists of a waist belt, two shoulder belts and a sword frog with steadying straps, the whole made from either black or brown curried buffalo leather. The furniture of the black belt is of nickel and that of the brown belt either brass or nickel.

The remaining accoutrements for use with the abovementioned belt are a pistol case and a "Sam Browne" ammunition pouch, which are also made from either black or brown leather with either brass or nickel furniture.

The waist belt is 2 inches wide and is made in three sizes. It is provided with a double tongued buckle, a stud, a flat sword hook, four dees secured to the upper edge for the attachment of the shoulder belts and two rectangular loops for the attachment of the frog. It is lined with thin cow leather for half its length.

The shoulder belt is $1\frac{1}{4}$-inch wide, tapering to $\frac{7}{8}$ inch $6\frac{3}{4}$ inches from the point, and is made in three sizes. A buckling piece with an oval buckle and one fixed and one running loop for adjusting the length of the belt, sewn to a billet filled with a stud and button-hole punched at the point, is fitted to the point end. The opposite end is provided with a billet with stud and button-hole punched at the point. The billets function with the dees on the waist belt.

The belt over the left shoulder need not be worn unless a revolver is carried.

The frog is provided with two adjustable suspending straps which function with the rectangular loops attached to the lower edge of the waist belt. Attached to the upper edge of the rear face of the frog is a small dee which functions over the sword hook on the waist belt when the sword is hooked up. A steadying strap punched at the point to function with the stud on the belt for steadying the sword belt is hooked through the dee and a stud is attached to the front face of the frog to function with the scabbard supporter.

The ammunition pouch and pistol case are provided with loops sewn to the back for attachment to the waist belt. They are both fastened by means of a tab and stud.

(b) Web sword belt.

This consists of a waist-belt and a shoulder suspender of web, strengthened at various parts with black morocco leather. It is furnished with loops, chapes, and dees. The loops and chapes are of morocco leather, and the furniture of gilding metal.

The suspender is fitted with hooks so that it can be removed when the belt is worn under the sash, outside the frock-coat.

(c) Sword-knot.

The sword-knot to be used with the brown "Sam Browne" waist belt is the "Knot, sword, brown, G. S." and that to be used with the black belt the "Knot, sword, black, D. S."

The former is a plain strap $\frac{5}{8}$ inch wide provided with a running loop, the ends of the strap being secured into an acorn covered with plaited leather. The length of the strap is 17 inches and the length of the acorn $2\frac{1}{4}$ inches.

The latter is a plaited strap provided with a plaited running loop, the ends of the strap being secured into an acorn covered with plaited leather. The length of the strap is 16 inches and the length of the acorn $2\frac{1}{4}$ inches.

(d) Web belt and bridle leather straps for carrying great-coat.

The belt is made from $2\frac{1}{2}$-inch web, and is strengthened at the eyelet holes by a light piece of leather. The coat straps are made from buff leather, and the furniture of gilding metal.

APPENDIX II.

REVOLVER.

Description of the latest pattern of service "Pistol, revolver, ·455" Webley Mk. VI".

This pistol belongs to the class of extracting revolvers. The calibre is ·441-inch. The principal parts are the barrel, which is 6 inches in length and fitted with a removable foresight and fixing screw, the cylinder, and the body.

The barrel is jointed to the body and held in position for firing by the rib extending back on to the body, and is firmly secured by the barrel catch, which has axis bosses formed on the inside faces.

The cylinder is chambered to hold 6 cartridges, and is mounted to the barrel on a fixed axis, and held in position at the time of extracting by the cam.

The stem of the extractor lies in the fixed axis, surrounded by a spiral spring which returns the extractor after ejecting the cartridge cases; the extractor is forced out by a small lever in the joint as the barrel is being rotated on the joint pin.

When it is necessary to remove the cylinder for cleaning, the fixing screw must be unscrewed, and the pistol opened to its fullest extent, then, by pressing the lever against the cam the cylinder will be free; in no other position can the cylinder be taken off the axis.

The body is fitted with a shield plate of hardened steel, to prevent wear of firing hole and to support base of cartridge.

The "Stocks, side, right and left," are fitted in two different sizes to suit different grips and are marked "M" (Medium), "S" (Small). "Protectors, hammer" can also be obtained to protect the hammer when undergoing snapping exercise.

Weight of pistol is 2 lbs. $6\frac{1}{4}$ ozs.

Cartridge charge, about $7\frac{1}{2}$ grains of cordite. Bullet, about 265 grains.

APPENDIX III.

Shoulder chains.

The rings must be made of the best hard drawn steel wire, which when faced together will make a diameter of ·065 inch. The external diameter of the rings to be ·4-inch. The chains are to contain 319 links, and weigh from 4 to $4\frac{1}{2}$ ozs.; they must be perfectly sound, well finished, and in all respects equal to the sealed pattern. The chain must resist a tensile strain of no less than 160 lbs., and the permanent elongation after such strain must not exceed $\frac{1}{16}$ inch over the full length of the shoulder chain. The breaking strain must be not less than 224 lbs., applied over the uniform width of 11 links, with attachments to 5 links so that weight is applied from end to end of the shoulder chain.

APPENDIX IV.

SWORDS, OFFICERS, INDIAN CAVALRY, SCABBARDS, SWORDS, OFFICERS, INDIAN CAVALRY.

Worn by officers of Indian cavalry, Bodyguards, Veterinary Corps and Army Remount Department.

Sword.—The blade of the sword is slightly curved, tapering gradually, 35 inches long from shoulder to point and is fullered on both sides commencing $1\frac{1}{2}$ inches from the

Appendices.

hilt to about 8¼ inches from the point. The blade is ornamentally embossed and bears the Royal Cypher and Crown also the manufacturer's name, and is nickel-plated.

The mountings consist of guard, grip, cupped ferrule, pommel and two nuts and are nickel-plated.

The guard is ornamentally embossed and bears the Royal Cypher and Crown.

The grip is of wood covered with fish skin, and bound with silver wire; the length varies from 5 inches to 5¾ inches. The variation being allowed to suit the size of the hand.

Swords of this pattern should stand the following tests:—

Blade.—In set and stiffened stage:—Struck on back and edge, and on both flats, on an oak block by hand.

With a weight of 34 lbs. in the vertical testing machine, the blade should recover straightness after not less than 1 inch depression; in the same machine, the blade should be shortened 4 inches, by bending from right to left, and then from left to right.

Hilt assembled.—Struck a moderate blow on an oak block, back and edge, to test the soundness of hilting.

Sword, complete.—With a weight of 32 lbs. in the vertical testing machine, it should recover straightness after not less than 1 inch depression.

Scabbard.—The scabbard is of steel, nickel-plated; it is fitted with a mouthpiece fixed to the scabbard with two small screws. Two bands with loose rings are brazed to the scabbard, 2¼ inches and 10½ inches respectively, from the top of the mouthpiece. The lining is of wood, one piece grooved which is water-roofed by soaking in white paraffin wax.

Length of sword	3 feet 5¾ inches.
„ „ scabbard	3 „ ½ inch.
„ „ blade from point to shoulder . . .	2 „ 11 inches.
Balance from hilt, about	3½ „
Weight of sword	2 lbs. 2 ozs.
„ „ scabbard	1 lb. 10 ozs.

SWORD, OFFICERS, RIFLE REGIMENTS SCABBARDS, SWORDS OFFICERS, RIFLE REGIMENTS.

Worn by officers of rifle regiments.

Sword.—The blade of the sword is straight, tapering gradually, it is $32\frac{9}{16}$ inches long from the shoulder to the point, and is fullered on both sides, commencing 2 inches from the shoulder to about 14½ inches from the point.

The mountings consist of guard, grip, ferrule, nut, strap and washer.

The guard, grip and ferrule are held in position by a nut screwed on the tang, underneath the strap; the trap is held by a washer, the end of the tang being riveted over the washer.

The guard is of malleable iron, or mild homogeneous steel, nickel-plated, ornamented with Royal Crown over the regimental device.

The grip is of wood covered with fish skin, and bound with silver wire; the length or the grip varies from 5 inches to 5¾ inches. The variation being allowed to suit the size of the hand.

The blade is ornamentally embossed and has the Royal Cypher and Crown also the manufacturer's name embossed. The guard, ferrule, strap and blade are nickel-plated.

Swords of this pattern should stand the following tests:—

Blade.—In set and stiffened stage—struck back and edge and on both flats, on an oak block by hand.

With a weight of 17 lbs. in the vertical testing machine, the blade should recover straightness after not less than 1 inch depression; in the same machine, the blade should be shortened 4 inches by bending from right to left and then left to right.

Hilt assembled.—Struck a moderate blow on an oak block, to test the soundness of the hilting.

Sword, complete.—With a weight of 15 lbs. in the vertical testing machine, it should recover straightness after not less than 1 inch depression.

Scabbard.—The scabbard is of steel, nickel-plated; it is fitted with a German silver mouthpiece with the sputcheon brazed on and fixed to the scabbard with two screws. Two bands with loose rings are brazed on to the scabbard $2\frac{3}{16}$ inches and $10\frac{3}{8}$ inches respectively, from the top of the mouthpiece. The lining consists of two wood strips held in position by the sputcheon.

Length of sword	. . . .	3 feet $2\frac{1}{4}$ inches.
,, ,, scabbard	. . . .	2 ,, $9\frac{3}{4}$,,
,, ,, blades from shoulder to point	. . .	2 ,, $8\frac{9}{16}$,,
Weight of sword	. . . .	1 lb. 12 ozs.
,, ,, scabbard	. . . .	1 lb. 1 oz.

SWORDS, OFFICERS, INDIAN ARMY; SCABBARDS, SWORDS, OFFICERS, INDIAN ARMY.

Worn by officers of infantry except where otherwise stated, Engineers, Sappers and Miners, Signals, Medical Services, Indian Army Service Corps, Indian Army Ordnance Corps, Military Farms Department, Military Engineer Services, Army Educational Services, Indian Miscellaneous List.

Sword.—The blade is straight tapering gradually, $32\frac{9}{16}$ inches long from shoulder to point and is fullered on both sides $1\frac{1}{4}$ inches from the guard for a total distance of 1 ft. $4\frac{1}{4}$ inches. The thickness of fullering to be not less than ·05 inch.

The mountings consist of guard, grip, ferrule, nut, strap and washer.

The guard, grip and ferrule are held in position by a nut screwed on the tang, underneath the strap; the strap is held by a washer, the end of the tang being riveted over the washer.

The guard is of steel and pierced with an ornamental device with the Royal Imperial Cypher on the outer boss of the hilt.

The grip is of wood covered with fish skin and bound with silver wire, the length of the grip varies from $5\frac{1}{4}$ inches to $5\frac{3}{4}$ inches to suit the size of the hand.

The blade is ornamentally embossed and bears the Royal Cypher and Crown and Manufacturer's name. The blade is nickel-plated. The guard, ferrule and strap are also nickel-plated.

Swords of this pattern should stand the following tests:—

Blade.—In set and stiffened stage—struck on back and edge and on both flats, on an oak block by hand.

With a weight of 34 lbs. in the vertical testing machine, the blade should recover straightness after not less than 1 inch depression, in the same machine, the blade should be shortened 4 inches, by bending from right to left and from left to right.

Hilt assembled.—Struck a moderate blow on an oak block, back and edge, to test the soundness of hilting.

Sword, complete.—With a weight of 32 lbs. in the vertical testing machine it should recover straightness after not less than 1 inch depression.

Scabbard.—The scabbard is steel, nickel-plated; it is fitted with a mouthpiece with the sputcheon brazed on to the scabbard with two small screws. Two bands with loose rings are brazed to the scabbard 2⅛ inches and 10⅜ inches respectively from the top of the mouthpiece. The lining consists of two strips of wood held in position under the sputcheon.

Length of sword	. . . .	3 feet $2\frac{3}{16}$ inches.
,, ,, scabbard	. . . .	2 ,, 10 ,,
,, ,, blade from point to shoulder	. . .	2 ,, $8\frac{9}{16}$,,
,, ,, sword and scabbard	. . . . .	3 ,, 4¾ ,,
Weight of sword	. . . .	2 lbs. 1½ ozs.
,, ,, scabbard	. . . .	14 ozs.

SWORDS, OFFICERS, ROYAL ARTILLERY, SCABBARDS, SWORDS, OFFICERS, ROYAL ARTILLERY.

Worn by officers of artillery.

Sword.—The blade is slightly curved, tapers gradually, is 35 inches long from shoulder to point, and is fullered on both sides, commencing 1½ inches from hilt, to about 9 inches from point, to a thickness of not less than ·04 inch.

The mountings consist of guard, grip, ferrule, strap, nut and washer.

The guard, grip and ferrule are held in position by a nut screwed on the tang underneath the strap ; the strap is held by a washer, the end of the tang being riveted over the washer.

The guard is of stamped mild steel of bar pattern.

The grip is of wood covered with fish skin and bound with silver wire, the length of the grip must be from 5 inches to 5¾ inches long to suit the size of the hand.

The blade may be plain or ornamentally embossed. In the latter case while it is not necessary that a uniform pattern of ornamentation should be followed, the design should not include any badge or device beyond the Royal Cypher and Crown, the R. A. badge embossed and the words "ROYAL ARTILLERY" and the usual manufacturer's name or trade mark.

Swords of this pattern should stand the following tests :—

Blade.—In set and stiffened stage—struck on back and edge, and on both flats, on an oak block by hand.

With a weight of 26 lbs. in the vertical testing machine, the blade should recover straightness after not less than 1 inch depression, in the same machine it should be shortened 4½ inches by bending from right to left, and then left to right.

Hilt assembled.—Struck a moderate blow on an oak block, back and edge, to test the soundness of hilting.

Sword, complete.—With a weight of 24 lbs. in the vertical testing machine, it should recover straightness after not less than 1 inch depression.

Scabbard.—The scabbard is of steel; it is fitted with a German-silver mouthpiece with the sputcheon brazed on, fixed to the scabbard with two screws ; two bands with loose rings are brazed to the scabbard, 2¼ inches and 10½ inches respectively from the top of the mouthpiece. The lining is of leather, blocked flesh side outturned, butted, and herring-bone stitched with fine waxed thread on the right side of lining, and held in position by the sputcheon.

Length of sword	. . . .	3 feet 5¼ inches.
,, ,, scabbard	. . . .	2 ,, 11⅞ ,,
,, ,, blade from shoulder to point	. . .	2 ,, 11 ,,
,, ,, sword and scabbard	. . . . .	3 ,, 6⅛ ,,
,, ,, balance from hilt, about	. . . .	5½ ,,
Weight of sword	. . . .	2 lbs.
,, ,, scabbard	. . . .	15¼ ozs.
,, ,, lining	. . . .	1½ ozs.

Scabbards for use with the "Sam Browne" belt.

The various scabbards are—

Scabbards, sword "Sam Browne".

   (i) Dismounted services.
   (ii) Mounted services.
   (iii) Highland regiments.
   (iv) R. A. officers.

Each scabbard is built up with two strips of wood grooved to receive the blade of the sword, butted and glued together, and covered with leather stitched down one side. It is provided with a leather shoe and a nickel-plated locket. A raised rib is formed below the locket by a piece of packing secured between the wood lining and the leather covering; the function of the rib is to prevent the scabbard slipping down through the frog. Secured round the rib is a leather supporter, with a button-holed tab which functions with the stud on the front of the frog to prevent the scabbard being withdrawn with the sword.

The length and weight of each scabbard is—

   (i) 2 ft. 10 inches . . . . $8\frac{1}{2}$ ozs.
   (ii) 3 ft. $\frac{3}{8}$ inch . . . . $9\frac{1}{2}$ ozs.
   (iii) 2 ft. $9\frac{5}{8}$ inches . . . . 9 ozs.
   (iv) 3 ft. $\frac{1}{4}$ inch . . . . 10 ozs.

APPENDIX V.

WATER BOTTLE.

Description of the "Bottle, water, enamelled, Mark VI" with which officers are recommended to provide themselves.

The bottle is made of charcoal iron plate enamelled blue, shaped to fit the hip and covered with felt. It is 7 inches deep, $5\frac{1}{4}$ inches wide and $2\frac{1}{4}$ inches thick and the neck is $1\frac{1}{4}$ inches long, tapered from $\frac{13}{16}$ inch at the bottom to $\frac{7}{8}$ inch at the top, inside.

The stopper is a good quality wine cork with a metal cap and is fitted with a pin secured by a nut, and provided with an eye for the attachment of the cord which connects the stopper to the bottle. The opposite end of the cord is secured to the inside of the cover, round the neck of the bottle, by sewing.

The bottle is carried by means of the "carrier, water, bottle with shoulder strap" which consists of a body formed from three pieces of leather riveted together, and a shoulder strap. The shoulder strap consists of a $\frac{1}{2}$ inch adjustable strap with 2 inches of cotton web and is attached to the body of the carrier by two brass rings which are secured to the vertical portion of the body.

APPENDIX VI.

WARRANT OFFICERS.

British Army.

1. Classes I and II warrant officers of the British Army will wear the dress footwear and badges of rank laid down in the Home Regulations, except that the superior quality of clothing described therein for class I warrant officers is not yet authorised for supply in India. These warrant officers may wear such clothing in India and replace it by clothing of similar quality at their own expense if they so desire.

2. Class I warrant officers are permitted to alter their khaki drill frocks to approximate to the pattern worn by departmental warrant officers of the I. U. L. by adding two additional pockets. The closed collar will be retained.

Class I warrant officers of dismounted units may wear khaki drill breeches (with putties) on occasions when the authorised dress is "Trousers with putties".

The amendment to the jacket and the provision of the breeches will be carried out at the expense of the individual regimentally.

The garments will not be worn outside Indian limits.

All Class I warrant officers of a unit will be dressed alike.

Replacements in the field will be of the authorised patterns of jackets and trousers.

3. Warrant officers of cavalry regiments may be permitted at the discretion of the C. Os. of units, to wear metal badges of authorised regimental design as arm badges on their service dress jackets, provided that no expense to the State is incurred and the badges are obtained under regimental arrangements.

These badges will be worn on the right arm below the badge of rank.

4. Accoutrements and arms are shewn in the appropriate equipment regulations for the army in India.

Indian Army.

British.—Class I warrant officers of the Indian Army will wear the dress authorised for dismounted officers with the following exceptions:—

Badges of rank of gilding metal will be worn on the forearm as follows:—

Royal arms and wreath . . Assistant surgeons ranking as conductors, conductors, and first class staff serjeant majors.

Royal arms . . . . All other class I warrant officers.

Brown ankle boots and putties will be worn except as shewn below:—

Indian Army Service Corps
Military Farms Department } Brown ankle boots, leggings and jack spurs.

Indian Army Ordnance Corps . Brown ankle boots and leggings.

Mess dress and patrol jackets.—The provisions of these articles is optional. If provided, the badges of rank will be of gold embroidery on a blue ground (on a white ground in the case of the Indian Army Service Corps).

The wearing of uniform by warant officers proceeding home on transports on leave pending retirement is optional.

Indian.—Indian warrant officers will wear the same pattern garments as authorised for Indian officers holding the Viceroy's commission (see para. 67).

The badges of rank will be of gilding metal worn on the forearm as follows:—

Sub-assistant surgeons and
Veterinary assistant surgeons Royal arms and wreath.

APPENDIX VII.

List of units whose officers are permitted to wear boots, leggings and putties which differ from the authorised pattern or colour.

Units.	Differences authorised.
All Indian infantry units whose mess dress is rifle green (see paras. 161 and 165).	Boots, leggings and putties as prescribed in para. 18 (e) and 41 except that the colour will be black.
12th Frontier Force Regiment (except the 5th battalion).	
5th battalion (Queen Victoria's Own Corps of Guides) 12th Frontier Force Regiment.	Brown field boots for all officers.

APPENDIX VIII.

Details of mess dress and forage caps for Indian cavalry regiments.

Unit.	Jacket.	Overalls.	Waistcoat.	Forage cap.
1	2	3	4	5
Skinners Horse (1st Duke of York's Own Cavalry).	Yellow cloth, long waisted coming to a point behind, lined with white silk serge with white leather around inside of waist, fastening at the neck with hooks, gilt studs down front. Jacket edged with one-inch lancer lace, large gold gimp on collar seam, piping of black velvet down hind arm seam and through cuff and back seam, through square dummies at bottom. Piping of black velvet all round jacket including top of collar also inside of gold lace round edge. Collar and cuffs of black velvet, with two buttons on each sleeve. Shoulder cords of gold wire lancer pattern with black velvet underneath.	Blue cloth, with double ¾-inch yellow cloth stripes, ½-inch apart.	Black silk velvet, fastening at the throat, no gilt studs in front. Ornamented with large gold chain gimp and gold figuring braid, tunic olivets in front.	Blue cloth with yellow band and welts.
2nd Lancers (Gardners Horse).	Blue cloth, lancer pattern, long waisted coming to a point behind lined turquoise blue silk, fastening at the neck with a loop of gold braid, gilt studs down front. Jacket trimmed with gold lace and gold chain gimp. Light blue welting to back seams of body and sleeves. Collar and cuffs of light blue cloth. Shoulder cords gold wire. Badges of rank in silver embroidery.	Blue cloth with double ¾-inch primrose cloth stripes, ⅜-inch apart.	Light blue cloth, lancer pattern, with turquoise silk back, fastened with hooks and eyes. Gilt studs in front. Trimmed gold lace and braid. Two pockets trimmed gold braid.	Ditto.

Appendices. 71

3rd Cavalry	Blue cloth, no buttons on the front of the jacket or on cuffs, no gold braid or piping. Roll step collar of blue cloth with primrose silk facing on the lapel. Blue cloth pointed cuffs, 6 inches deep at the points and 2¾ inches behind. A 1 inch slit at the seam. Shoulder straps of blue cloth, 1¾ inches wide at the base tapering to about 1 inch at the points, rounded points fastened with a small button.	Blue cloth with double ¾-inch yellow cloth stripes, ½-inch apart.	White washing, open in front, no collar, fastened with four vest buttons.	Ditto.
Hodson's Horse (4th D. C. O. Lancers).	Blue cloth, long waisted, coming to a point behind, cut round over the hips, fastening up to the throat with hooks, but when worn open fastened by a loop of tracing braid, gilt studs down the front. Jacket edged all round and on cuffs with one-inch gold braid, scarlet piping in the sleeves and down the back seams, dummies at back seams. Collar and pointed cuffs of scarlet cloth with two buttons on each cuff. Badges of rank in gold embroidery.	Blue cloth with double ¾-inch red cloth stripes.	Scarlet cloth, fastening up to the throat with hooks. Gilt studs down the front. Front trimmed with 7/10-inch gold braid, with one row of gold braided eyes, five braided points and smaller points in between. Pockets cut straight and braided with gold braid having braided points at each end and one over and below, and three gold braided eyes in between each point.	Ditto.
Probyn's Horse (5th King Edwards Own Lancers).	Blue cloth, long waisted coming to a point behind, cut round over the hips, fastening up to the throat with hooks, but when worn open fastened with a loop of tracing braid, gilt studs down the front. Jacket trimmed with ¾-inch gold lace down the front, scarlet cloth piping in the sleeve and down the back seams, dummies at back seams. Collar and pointed cuffs of scarlet cloth, two buttons on each cuff. Shoulder cords of gold wire. Badges of rank in silver embroidery.	Blue cloth with double ¾-inch yellow cloth stripes, ½-inch apart.	Scarlet cloth, fastening up to the throat with hooks. Gilt studs down the front. Trimmed with gold lace.	Ditto.

APPENDIX VIII—contd.

Details of mess dress and forage caps for Indian cavalry regiments—contd.

Unit.	Jacket.	Overalls.	Waistcoat.	Forage cap.
1	2	3	4	5
6th (D. C. O.) Lancers	Blue cloth, lined scarlet silk, gilt studs down the front. Jacked edged all round and on cuffs with 1-inch gold lancer lace, scarlet cloth piping all round the jacket, on cuffs, hind arm, side body seams and on bottom of dummies. A line of gold chain gimp along collar seam. Collar of scarlet refine and cuffs of scarlet cloth, two flat gilt buttons on each cuff. Shoulder cords of gold wire lancer cord. Badges of rank in silver embroidery.	Blue cloth with double ¾-inch scarlet cloth stripes.	Scarlet refine, gilt studs down front. Braided with gold chain gimp and gold tracing braid. Edged all round with gold chain gimp forming seven eyes on front, one in bottom point and three along bottom edge. A line of eyes in tracing braid inside the gold chain gimp. Pockets cut straight and braided with double gold tracing braid forming crow's toes above, below and at the ends.	Blue cloth with scarlet band and welts.
7th Light Cavalry	Blue cloth, long waisted, coming to a point behind, cut round over the hips, fastening up to the throat with hooks, but when worn open fastened with a loop of tracing braid. Silver studs down the front. The jacket is laced with silver lace, piping of French grey cloth in the sleeves and down the back seams. Dummies at back seams. Silver chain gimp round bottom of collar. Collar and pointed cuffs of French grey cloth with two small buttons on each cuff. Shoulder cords of silver lancer cord." Badges of rank in silver embroidery.	Blue cloth with double ¾-inch French grey cloth stripes ¼-inch apart.	French grey cloth, trimmed with ¾-inch lancer silver lace and tracing braid.	Blue cloth with French grey band and welts.

8th (K. G. O.) Light Cavalry.	Blue cloth, long waisted, coming to a point behind, cut round over the hips, fastening up to the throat with hooks, but when worn open fastened with a loop of tracing braid, gilt studs down front. The jacket is laced with $\frac{1}{2}$-inch gold lace, piping of French grey cloth in the sleeves and down the back seams. Dummies at back seams. Gold chain gimp round bottom of collar. Collar and cuffs of French grey cloth with two small buttons on each cuff. Shoulder straps of twisted gold cord. Badges of rank in gold embroidery.	Ditto	White cloth, trimmed with $\frac{3}{8}$-inch lancer gold lace and tracing braid.	Ditto.
The Royal Deccan Horse (9th Horse).	Rifle green cloth, long waisted, coming to a point behind, cut round over the hips, lined with white twilled silk. Fastening up to the throat with hooks. Gilt studs down the front. The jacket is laced with $\frac{1}{2}$-inch gold lace, Collar and pointed cuffs of white cloth. Shoulder straps of $\frac{3}{4}$-inch gold lancer cord. Badges of rank in gold embroidery.	Rifle green cloth with double $\frac{3}{4}$-inch white cloth stripes $\frac{1}{4}$-inch apart.	White cloth, gilt studs down front. Edged with $\frac{3}{4}$-inch gold lancer lace and gold figuring braid on the fronts of the waistcoat.	Blue cloth with white band and welts.
The Guides Cavalry (10th Q. V. O. Frontier Force).	Drab cloth, long waisted, coming to a point behind, cut round over the hips, fastening up to the throat with hooks, no gilt studs down the front. Collar and pointed cuffs of red velvet. Shoulder straps of painted drab silk. Badges of rank in silver embroidery.	Drab cloth with double $\frac{3}{4}$-inch drab lace stripes, $\frac{1}{8}$th inch apart, with a light of red in between.	Scarlet cloth, fastening at the throat, gilt studs down the front. Trimmed with gold braid down the front and along the pockets.	Blue cloth with scarlet band and welts.
P. A. V. O. Cavalry (11th Frontier Force).	Blue cloth, long waisted, coming to a point behind, cut round over the hips, fastening up to the throat with hooks, gilt studs down the front. When worn open fastened with a loop of tracing braid at the throat. Jacket is edged with $\frac{1}{2}$-inch lace. Collar and cuffs of scarlet cloth with two buttons on each cuff. Shoulder straps of scarlet cloth edged with $\frac{1}{2}$-inch lace. Badges of rank in gold embroidery.	Blue cloth with double $\frac{3}{4}$-inch scarlet cloth stripes $\frac{1}{8}$-inch apart.	Scarlet cloth, fastening at the throat, gilt studs down the front.	Blue cloth with yellow band and welts.

APPENDIX VIII—contd.

Details of mess dress and forage caps for Indian cavalry regiments—contd.

Unit.	Jacket.	Overalls.	Waistcoat.	Forage cap.
1	2	3	4	5
Sam Browne's Cavalry (12th Frontier Force).	Scarlet cloth, long waisted, coming to a point behind, cut round over the hips, lined scarlet, fastened up the front with hooks and eyes. Worn open fastened with a loop of gold tracing braid at the throat. Gilt studs down front. Jacket is edged all round with ½-inch gold dragoon lace, large gold gimp on the base of the collar. Collar and cuffs of blue cloth, the cuffs pointed with 1-inch gold lace. Two small gilt ball buttons on each sleeve above the cuffs. Shoulder straps of large gold chain gimp fastened with a small half ball button, gilt. Badges of rank in silver embroidery.	Blue cloth with double ¾-inch stripes of yellow cloth ⅛-inch apart.	Scarlet refine. Edged all round with ⅜-inch lace, single scallop. Fronts braided with gold tracing braid.	Blue cloth with scarlet band and welts.
13th D. C. O. Lancers	Blue cloth, lined scarlet, Gilt studs down front. Jacket is edged with 1-inch gold lace, double scallop, chain gimp along collar seam. Piped all round on cuffs, on hind arm seam and side body seams with scarlet cloth. Collar and cuffs of scarlet refine, the cuffs edged with 1-inch gold lace (double scallop). Two buttons on each cuff. Shoulder straps of gold wire lancer cord fastened with a small button. Badges of rank in gold embroidery.	Blue cloth with double ¾-inch scarlet cloth stripes ⅛-inch apart.	Scarlet cloth, fastening up to the throat with hooks. Gilt studs down the front. Trimmed with ½-inch lace.	Ditto.

Appendices. 75

Scindo Horse (14th P. W. O. Cavalry).	Dark blue cloth, long waisted, coming to a point behind, cut round over the hips, fastened up to the front with hooks, gilt studs down the front. When worn open fastened with a loop of tracing braid at the throat. Jacket and collar edged with ¾-inch gold lace, gimp at the base of the collar. Double gold tracing braid at back seams, terminating at sleeves with treble eyes and at waist with two embroidered frogs. Collar and pointed cuffs of scarlet cloth edged with ¼-inch gold lace. Shoulder straps of plaited gold chain gimp lined blue. Badges of rank in gold embroidery.	Ditto . . .	Ditto . . .	Ditto.
15th Lancers	Dark blue cloth, long waisted, coming to a point behind, cut round over the hips, fastening up the front with hooks, gilt studs down the front. When worn open fastened with a loop of tracing braid at the throat. Jacket and collar edged with 1-inch gold lancer lace, gimp at the base of the collar. Buff piping on back seams and sleeves terminating at the waist with two embroidered frogs. Collar and pointed cuffs of buff cloth edged with 1-inch gold lancer lace. Shoulder straps of gold lancer wire. Badges of rank in silver embroidery.	Blue cloth with double ¾-inch buff cloth stripes ¼-inch apart.	Buff cloth, with five ball buttons and gimp scroll lace. Trimmed with ¾-inch gold lancer lace and single stripes braid. Two pockets outlined in gold braid.	Bule cloth with buff band and welts.
16th Light Cavalry	Dark blue cloth, long waisted, coming to a point behind, cut round over the hips, lined grey Italian throughout. Silver studs down the front. Worn open fastened with a loop of silver tracing braid at bottom of the collar. Jacket and collar edged with 1-inch lancer pattern silver lace, one row of silver chain	Dark blue with double ¼-inch French grey cloth stripes, ¼-inch apart.	French grey cloth, fastened up to the throat, silver studs down the front. Back of grey Italian cloth, lined white cotton. Lancer pattern silver ¾-inch lace one row down front edges and bottom of fronts and on collar.	Blue cloth with French grey band and welts.

APPENDIX VIII—concld.

Details of mess dress and forage caps for Indian cavalry regiments—concld.

Unit.	Jacket.	Overalls.	Waistcoat.	Forage cap.
1	2	3	4	5
16th Light Cavalry—*contd.*	gimp lace round bottom of collar. One row of French grey piping on back seams and behind seams of sleeves. Dummies of silver lace at bottom of back seams. Collar and pointed cuffs of French grey cloth. Cuffs trimmed with one row of 1-inch silver lace with two small buttons above the lace. Shoulder cords of lancer pattern silver wire, fastened with screw socket button and tapes. Badges of rank in gold embroidery.		One row silver tracing braid round collar in loops. Fronts and pockets trimmed silver tracing braid.	
The Poona Horse (17th Q. V. O. Cavalry).	Blue cloth, gilt studs down the front. Collar fastened with a loop of small gold braid and collar. Jacket trimmed with 1-inch gold lace, base of collar trimmed with large chain gold gimp. Double tracing braid down back seams of jacket. Collar and cuffs of French grey cloth. Shoulder cords of large gold chain gimp. Badges of rank in silver embroidery lined with French grey silk.	Blue cloth with double ¾-inch French grey cloth stripes ½-inch apart.	French grey cloth, gilt studs down front. Trimmed with ¼-inch gold lace.	Blue cloth with scarlet band and welts.
18th (K. E. O.) Cavalry	Blue cloth, lined white. Hooks and eyes down the front. Gilt studs. Jacket edged all round with ⅜-inch lace. Collars and cuffs of French grey cloth. Collar seam covered with chain gimp. Cuffs edged with ½-inch gold lace. Shoulder straps of French grey cloth covered with gold cord. Badges of rank in gold embroidery.	Ditto	French grey cloth, hooks and eyes in front, fastened with oviletle buttons and chain gimp straps. Edged with ½-inch gold lace.	Ditto.

Appendices.

Regiment			
19th K. G. O. Lancers	Scarlet cloth, long waisted, coming to a point behind, cut round over the hips, fastening up to the throat with hooks, gilt studs down the front. Lined white. When worn open fastened with a loop of gold braid. Jacket is trimmed with ¾-inch gold chain gimp. Dummies at back seams trimmed with gold lace. Hind arm of sleeves and side body piped with white cloth piping. Collar and pointed cuffs of white cloth with two buttons on each cuff. Shoulder straps of gold wire. Badges of rank in silver embroidery.	Blue cloth with double ¾-inch white cloth stripes, ½-inch apart.	White cloth, fastening at the throat with hooks and eyes. Gilt studs down the front. Trimmed ¾-inch gold chain gimp to top of collar seam only and down front and round the bottom with 11 loops. Pockets trimmed with 8 loops.	Blue cloth with white band and welts.
20th Lancers	Blue cloth, long waisted, coming to a point behind, cut round over the hips, fastening up to the throat with hooks, gilt studs down the front. When worn open fastened with a loop of tracing braid. Jacket is trimmed with 1-inch gold lace down the fronts, scarlet piping in the sleeve and down the back seams. Dummies at back seams. Collar and pointed cuffs of scarlet cloth. Shoulder straps of plaited gold cord. Badges of rank in gold embroidery.	Blue cloth with double ¾-inch scarlet cloth stripes, ¼-inch apart, with lancer piping in between.	Scarlet cloth, fastening to the throat with hooks. Four buttons down the front. Trimmed with narrow gold lace round edge and edge of pockets, and with gold embroidery design inside that.	Field pattern, blue cloth sides with red top and white centre sides edged with gold piping.
The Central India Horse (21st K. G. O. Lancers).	Drab cloth, fastened with hooks and eyes: gilt studs down the front. Lined drab silk. Maroon velvet piping round collar, bottom edge and cuffs. No piping on front. Collar and cuffs of maroon velvet 1-inch gold dragoon lace on cuffs and two small buttons at back of cuffs. A line of large chain gimp along bottom of collar, with gold braid loops on collar. Shoulder straps of large chain gimp fastened with a small button. Badges of rank in silver embroidery.	Drab cloth with double maroon cloth stripes ¾-inch wide, ¼-inch apart.	Drab cloth, fastened with hooks and eyes. Gilt studs down the front. Trimmed maroon piping all round and on pockets; ¾-inch gold dragoon lace all round; gold Russia braid formed in ½-inch eyes all round except on back of collar where it is straight, gold Russia braid on pockets.	Drab cloth with maroon band welt around the crown.

APPENDIX IX.

Badges and devices, Indian cavalry.

Regiment.	On buttons.	On collar of tunic and mess jacket.	On collar of service dress.	On head-dress (helmet, pagri, or felt hat).	On cap.
1	2	3	4	5	6
Skinner's Horse (1st Duke of York's Own Cavalry).	In brass, crossed lances, bearing pennons. Duke of York's rose at the crossing of the lances.	In brass, crossed lances, bearing pennons, Duke of York's rose, in white metal, at the crossing of the lances, and crown above. Below a scroll inscribed "Himmat-i-Mardan Madad-i-Khuda".	As in column (3)	*Nil*	As in column (3).
2nd Lancers (Gardner's Horse).	*Service dress.*—Brown leather buttons (stamped knot). *Tunic and mess dress.*—In gilding metal crossed lances bearing pennons; in upper angle a crown. Monogram "B. L." at the crossing of the lances.	In silver, crossed lances, bearing pennons; in upper angle a lion passant regardant. A crown at the crossing of the lances; the figure "2" in the lower angle with a scroll below inscribed "Scinde".	As in column (3) but in bronze.	*Nil*	As in column (3) but larger.
3rd Cavalry	Plain gilding metal buttons	In silver, crossed swords; in upper angle a crown and the figure "III" at the crossing of the swords. Below a scroll inscribed "Cavalry".	*Nil*	*Nil*	As in column (3) but larger and in silver.
Hodson's Horse (4th D. C. O. Lancers).	In gilding metal, crossed lances bearing pennons; a crown in upper angle and the letter "H" in side angles.	In silver, crossed lances, bearing pennons; a crown in upper angle and below a scroll inscribed "Hodson's Horse".	As in column (3)	*Nil*	As in column (3) but larger.

Appendices.

Regiment	(Column 2)	(Column 3)	(Column 4)	(Column 5)	(Column 6)
Probyn's Horse (5th King Edward's Own Lancers).	In gilding metal, crossed lances with pennons; the Prince of Wales' plume and motto at the crossing of the lances; below, resting on the lances, a scroll inscribed "Probyn's Horse".		In silver, the plume of the Prince of Wales.	Nil.	In silver, the design as in column (2).
6th (D. C. O.) Lancers	In gilding metal, crossed lances, bearing pennons and "6" at the crossing of the lances.	*On collar of mess jacket only.*—In silver, crossed lances bearing pennons and the figure "6" at the crossing of the lances. Below a scroll inscribed "The Duke of Connaught's Own".	In bronze as in column (3).	Nil	In gilding metal as in column (3) but larger.
7th Light Cavalry	Silver buttons, device as in column (3).	In silver, crossed lances, bearing pennons, in upper angle a crown and the figure "7" at the crossing of the lances.	As in column (3)	Nil	As in column (3) but larger.
8th (K. G. O.) Light Cavalry.	Plain silver buttons	In silver, crossed lances, bearing pennons; in upper angle a crown and the figure "8", at the crossing of the lances. Letters "K. G. O." in lower angle.	As in column (3)	Nil	As in column (3) but larger.
9th The Royal Deccan Horse (9th Horse).	Gilding metal buttons, device as in column (3).	In silver, crossed lances, bearing pennons. Letters "R. D. H." at the crossing of the lances and encircled by a garter inscribed "Honi Soit Qui Mal y Pense". Below a scroll inscribed "Royal Deccan Horse". The whole surmounted by a crown.	As in column (3)	Nil	As in column (3) but larger.

APPENDIX IX—contd.

Badges and devices, Indian cavalry—contd.

Regiment.	On buttons.	On collar of tunic and mess jacket.	On collar of service dress.	On head-dress (helmet, pagri, or felt hat).	On cap.
1	2	3	4	5	6
The Guides Cavalry (10th Q. O. F. F.).	Plain silver buttons	Nil	Nil	Nil	In silver, the cypher of Queen Victoria within a Garter inscribed "Honi Soit Qui Mal y Pense" and surmounted by a crown. The whole surrounded by a scroll bearing the words "Queen Victoria's Own Corps of Guides".
P. A. V. O. Cavalry (11th F. F.).	Plain gilding metal buttons	In silver, the Kandahar Star upon two crossed swords, surmounted by a crown; in the centre "P. A. V. O." encircled by a band inscribed "Kabul to Kandahar 1880".	As in column (3) but in gilding metal.	Nil	As in column (4) but larger.
Sam Browne's Cavalry (12th Frontier Force).	Plain gilding metal buttons	Nil	Nil	*On helmet only.*—In silver, an Indian horseman carrying a sword encircled by a stirrup leather inscribed "Sam Browne's	As in column (5).

Appendices. 81

13th D. C. O. Lancers	In gilding metal, crossed lances, bearing pennons; in upper angle a crown. Monogram "D. C. O." at the crossing of the lances.	Crossed lances bearing pennons, in upper angle a crown. The figure "13th" at the crossing of the lances. Below a scroll inscribed "Duke of Connaught's Own". Numerals in silver; remainder gilt.	As in column (3)	*On helmet only.*—A hackle (plume of black cock feathers) with the same badge as in column (3).	As in column (3) but larger.
Scinde Horse (14th P. W. O. Cavalry).	Gilding metal buttons charged with the plume of the Prince of Wales in white metal. The letters "S" and "H" on the left and right side respectively of the plume.	In silver, an Indian horseman bearing a lance with a scroll below inscribed "P. W. O. The Scinde Horse".	As in column (3)	*Nil*	As in column (3) but larger.
15th Lancers	"XV" on a plain round gilding metal button.	In silver, crossed lances, bearing pennons and "XV" at the crossing of the lancers. Below a scroll inscribed "Lancers".	As in column (3) but larger and in gilding metal.	*Nil*	As in column (3) but larger and in gilding metal on the service dress cap.
16th Light Cavalry	In white metal, crossed lances bearing pennons with the figure "16" at the crossing of the lances. In the upper angle a crown and in the lower angle the letters "L. C.".	*Nil*	In silver, crossed lances, bearing pennons with the figure "16" at the crossing. In upper angle a crown and below a scroll inscribed "Light Cavalry".	*Nil*	As in column (4) but larger.

APPENDIX IX—concld.

Badges and devices, Indian cavalry—concld.

Regiment.	On buttons.	On collar of tunic and mess jacket.	On collar of service dress.	On head-dress (helmet, pagri, or felt hat).	On cap.
1	2	3	4	5	6
The Poona Horse (17th Queen Victoria's Own Cavalry).	*Service dress.*—In gilding metal the Royal and Imperial Cypher of Queen Victoria within the Garter surmounted by a Tudor crown. Below a scroll bearing the words "Queen Victoria's Own Poona Horse". *Mess dress.*—In gilding metal with the Royal and Imperial Cypher of Queen Victoria within the Garter surmounted by a Tudor crown embossed in silver.	*On collar of mess jacket only.*—In silver the Royal and Imperial Cypher of Queen Victoria within the Garter surmounted by a Tudor crown. Below a scroll bearing the words "Queen Victoria's Own Poona Horse".	*Nil*	*Nil*	As in column (3) but larger.
18th (K. E. O.) Cavalry.	*Service dress.*—Leather buttons. *For all other dress.*—Front buttons—brass olivette. For pockets and shoulders straps—gilding metal charged with the plume of the Prince of Wales in silver, surmounted by a crown the figures "1" and "8" on the left and right side, respectively, of the plume, the letters "K. E. O. Cavalry" at the base.	In silver, the Royal and Imperial Cypher of King Edward VII, surmounted by a gilt crown. Below a scroll inscribed "K. E. O. 18th Cavalry" scroll in gilt—numerals and lettering in silver.	As in column (3)	*Nil*	In gilt-crossed lances, bearing pennons, in upper angle the plume of the Prince of Wales in silver with the coroneting gilt, the figure "18" in the centre and a scroll below inscribed "K. E. O. Cavalry".

Appendices.

19th (K. G. O.) Lancers.	Gilding metal charged with the plume of the Prince of Wales in white metal.	The plume of the Prince of Wales in metal.	As in column (3)	In gilding metal, crossed lances with pennons, in upper angle the figure "19" surmounted by a crown the letters "G. R. I." at the crossing of the lances. Below a scroll inscribed "King George's Own Lancers".
20th Lancers .	Gilding metal buttons device as in column (3).	*Nil*	In gilding metal (silver on mess jacket), crossed lances, bearing pennons with a crown at the crossing of the lances. "XX" in roman figures in the lower angle with a scroll below inscribed "Lancers".	As in column (3) but larger.
The Central India Horse (21st K. G. O. Lancers).	Gilding metal buttons device as in column (3).	*On helmet*—In gilding metal, the plume of the Prince of Wales.	In silver, crossed lances bearing pennons; in upper angle a crown. Monogram "C. I. H." at the crossing of the lances.	As in column (3) but larger.

APPENDIX X.

Details of mess dress and forage caps for Indian Pioneers and infantry.

Unit.	Jacket.	Overalls.	Waistcoat.	Forage cap.
The Corps of Madras Pioneers.	Scarlet cloth. Roll collar of white cloth. Pointed cuffs of white cloth, 6 inches deep at the points and 2¾ inches behind. 1-inch slit at the seams. Shoulder straps of white cloth, 1¾ inches at the base tapering to about 1 inch at the points: rounded points fastened with a small button, sewn in at the shoulder. Badges of rank in metal.	Blue cloth with a scarlet welt ¼-inch wide down the side seams.	White washing, open in front, no collar, fastened with four vest buttons.	Blue cloth with black oakleaf lace band and a scarlet welt round the crown.
The Corps of Bombay Pioneers.	Scarlet cloth. The jacket, cuffs, collar and shoulder straps edged with white piping. Roll collar of white cloth. Pointed cuffs of white cloth, 6 inches deep at the points and 3¾ inches behind. 1 inch slit at the seam. Shoulder straps of white cloth, 1¾ inches at the base tapering to about 1 inch at the points: rounded points fastened with a small button, sewn in at the shoulder. Badges of rank in metal.	Blue cloth with a scarlet welt ¼-inch wide down the side seams.	White washing, open in front, no collar, fastened with four vest buttons.	Blue cloth with black oakleaf lace band and a scarlet welt round the crown.
The Corps of Sikh Pioneers.	Scarlet cloth, four buttons down the front of the jacket. The jacket, cuffs, collar and shoulder straps edged with white piping. Roll collar of blue cloth. Pointed cuffs of white cloth, 6 inches deep at the points and 2¾ inches behind. 1-inch slit at the seams.	Blue cloth with a scarlet welt ¼-inch wide down the side seams.	Dark blue cloth, open in front, no collar, fastened with four vest buttons.	Blue cloth with black oakleaf lace band and a scarlet welt round the crown.

The Corps of Hazara Pioneers.	Shoulder straps of blue cloth, 1¾ inches wide at the base tapering to about 1 inch at the points; rounded points fastened with a small button; sewn in at the shoulder. Badges of rank in metal.	
	Scarlet cloth. Roll collar of plum coloured silk. Pointed cuffs of scarlet cloth, 6 inches deep at the points and 2¾ inches behind. 1-inch slit at the seams. Shoulder straps of scarlet cloth, 1¾ inches wide at the base tapering to about 1 inch at the points; rounded points fastened with a small button; sewn in at the shoulder. Badges of rank in metal.	Ditto.	White washing, open in front, no collar, fastened with four vest buttons.	Ditto.
1st Punjab Regiment.	Scarlet cloth. Roll collar of grass green cloth. Pointed cuffs of grass green cloth, 6 inches deep at the points and 2¾ inches behind. 1-inch slit at the seams. Shoulder straps of scarlet cloth, 1¾ inches at the base tapering to about 1 inch at the points; rounded points fastened with a small button; sewn in at the shoulder. Badges of rank in gold embroidery.	Ditto.	Ditto.	Ditto.
2nd Punjab Regiment.	Scarlet cloth. Roll collar of grass green cloth. Pointed cuffs of grass green cloth, 6 inches deep at the points and 2¾ inches behind. 1-inch slit at the seams. Shoulder straps of grass green cloth, 1¾ inches at the base tapering to about 1 inch at the points; rounded points fastened with a small button; sewn in at the shoulder. Badges of rank in metal.	Ditto.	Ditto.	Ditto.

APPENDIX X—contd.

Details of mess dress and forage caps for Indian Pioneers and infantry—contd.

Unit.	Jacket.	Overalls.	Waistcoat.	Forage cap.
4th Bombay Grenadiers.	Scarlet cloth. Roll collar of white cloth. Pointed cuffs of white cloth, 6 inches deep at the points, 2¾ inches behind. 1-inch slit at the seams. Shoulder straps of white cloth, 1¾ inches wide at the base tapering to about 1 inch at the points; rounded points fastened with a small button; sewn in at the shoulders. Badges of rank in metal.	Blue cloth with a scarlet welt ¼-inch wide down the side seams.	White washing, open in front, no collar, fastened with four vest buttons.	Blue cloth with black oakleaf lace band and a scarlet welt round the crown.
5th Mahratta Light Infantry.	Scarlet cloth, three buttons down the front of the jacket. The jacket, cuffs, collar and shoulder straps edged with white piping. Roll collar of black cloth. Pointed cuffs of black cloth, 6 inches deep at the points and 2¾ inches behind. 1-inch slit at the seams. Two buttons on each cuff. Shoulder straps of black cloth, 1¾ inches at the base tapering to about 1 inch at the points; rounded points fastened with a small button; sewn in at the shoulder. Badges of rank in metal.	Ditto	Ditto	Blue cloth with black oakleaf lace band and scarlet welt round the crown. *Sanctioned as a temporary measure—*fatigue cap, blue cloth with white piping.
6th Rajputana Rifles.	Rifle green cloth, stand up collar. Body, except collar, trimmed with black mohair braid all round forming barrels (or dummies) at the bottom of the side seams. Side seams trimmed with double ¼-inch mohair braid forming a crow's foot at the top. Five wavy drop loops with single eyes at the outer ends, two rows of olivettes	Rifle green cloth with a single 2-inch black braid strips down the side seams.	Rifle green cloth, no collar, open half way down, fastened with hooks and eyes. Trimmed with two lines of seams ¾-inch black mohair braid down the front with ¼-inch scarlet cloth between with figuring of single eyes on top of the scarlet.	Rifle green with black mohair braid band and a black welt round the crown.

Appendices.

7th Rajput Regiment.	at both sides. Pockets trimmed with ½-inch mohair braid forming three eyes in the centre above and below, and crows foot at both ends. Collar of scarlet cloth with ½-inch mohair braid all round with figuring inside. Pointed cuffs of scarlet cloth, with 1-inch mohair braid, figuring of black Russia braid above, and inside braid forming a crows foot at the point. Shoulder straps of black chain gimp, rifle regiment pattern. Badges of rank in black. Scarlet cloth. The jacket, cuffs, collar and shoulder straps edged with white piping. Roll collar of yellow cloth (royal blue for the 1st Battalion). Pointed cuffs of yellow cloth (royal blue for the 1st Battalion) 6 inches deep behind the points and 2¾ inches behind. 1-inch slit at the seams. Shoulder straps of yellow cloth (royal blue in the case of the 1st Battalion), 1¾ inches wide at the base tapering to about 1 inch at the points; rounded points fastened with a small button; sewn in at the shoulder. Badges of rank in metal.	Blue cloth, with a scarlet welt ¼-inch wide down the side seams.	Pockets trimmed with ¼ inch braid underlaid with scarlet cloth shewing a narrow edge of scarlet on both sides of the braid, crows foot at ends. White washing (royal blue for the 1st Battalion), open in front, no collar, fastened with four vest buttons.	Blue cloth with black oakleaf lace band and a scarlet welt round the crown.
8th Punjab Regiment.	Drab cloth. Roll collar of blue cloth. Pointed cuffs of blue cloth, 6 inches deep at the points and 2¾ inches behind. 1-inch slit at the seams. Shoulder straps of drab cloth, 1¾ inches wide at the base tapering to about 1 inch at the points; rounded points fastened with a small button; sewn in at the shoulder. Badges of rank in metal.	Drab cloth with a single 2-inch mohair braid stripe down the side seams.	Drab cloth, open in front, no vest collar, fastened with four buttons.	Drab cloth with drab mohair braid band and a blue welt round the crown.

APPENDIX X—contd.

Details of mess dress and forage caps for Indian Pioneers and infantry—contd.

Unit.	Jacket.	Overalls.	Waistcoat.	Forage cap.
9th Jat Regiment	Scarlet cloth, 4 buttons down the front of the jacket. Roll collar of blue cloth. Pointed cuffs of blue cloth, 6 inches deep at the points and 2¾ inches behind. 1 inch slit at the seams. Two buttons on each cuff. Shoulder straps of blue cloth, 1¾ inches wide at the base tapering to about 1-inch at the points; rounded points fastened with a small button; sewn in at the shoulder. Badges of rank in metal.	Blue cloth with a scarlet welt ¼-inch wide down the side seams.	White washing, open in front, no collar, fastened with four vest buttons.	Blue cloth with black oakleaf lace band and a scarlet welt round the crown.
10th Baluch Regiment	Rifle green cloth with stand up collar, fastened at the neck with a loop of braid and one hook and eye. Black studs down the left edge. Body trimmed with black square cord all round the edging. Collar of cherry red cloth, trimmed all round with ½-inch black mohair braid with a tracing of rings in black mohair tracing braid forming a ring in each bottom corner of the collar. Centre of collar trimmed with plumes in balck mohair tracing braid. Pointed cuffs of cherry red cloth with tracing of black braid forming small row of eyes all round top edge. Shoulder straps of black chain gimp. Badges of rank in black metal with red cloth edging.	Baluch red	Rifle green cloth, no collar, open half way down, fastened with hooks and eyes. Trimmed with ½-inch mohair braid down the edge and around the bottom, with another row 1 inch from the edge. Row of small eyes of black tracing braid (plain) all round the inside forming a small eye at the bottom corners. Pockets trimmed with ¼-inch mohair braid forming a crow's foot at each end. Baluch red cloth under the front braiding and pockets.	Rifle green cloth with black mohair band and a black welt round the crown.

Appendices. 89

11th Sikh Regiment	Scarlet cloth. The jacket, cuffs, collar and shoulder straps edged with white piping. Roll collar of yellow cloth (emerald green for the second battalion). Pointed cuffs of yellow cloth (emerald green for the second battalion) 6-inch deep at the points and 2¾-inch behind, 1-inch slit at the seams. Shoulder straps of yellow cloth (emerald green for the second battalion) 1½-inch wide at the base tapering to about 1-inch at the points; rounded points fastened with a small button; sewn in at the shoulder. Badges of rank in metal.	Blue cloth with a scarlet welt ¼-inch wide down the side seams.	White washing (emerald green for the second battalion) open in front, no collar, fastened with four vest buttons.	Blue cloth with black oakleaf lace band and a scarlet welt round the crown.
12th Frontier Force Regiment.	Drab cloth, long waisted, coming to a point behind, cut round over the hips, fastening up to the throat with hooks, no studs down the front. Jacket edged with ¼-inch lace. On the sleeves a knot of square drab cloth (of the old Bengal cavalry pattern) traced all round with six small eyes, two at the bottom, two at the centre and two at the top with a crows foot at the extreme top and one at the bottom on the cuff. Collar and cuffs of red velvet. Shoulder cords of plaited drab silk. Badges of rank in silver embroidery.	Drab cloth with double ⅜-inch drab lace stripes, with a red welt between the stripes.	*All battalions except the 5th.—* Scarlet cloth, open in front, no collar, fastened with four vest buttons. Trimmed with gold braid around edge, down the fronts and along the pockets. *5th Battalion only.—* Scarlet cloth, fastened up to the throat. Gilt studs down front. Trimmed with gold braid, Gold braid along the pockets.	Drab cloth with drab cloth band and a red welt round the crown.
13th Frontier Force Regiment.	Rifle green cloth, with stand up collar, hooks and eyes down the front. Jacket trimmed with four loops of black square cord with netted caps and drops fastening with black olivets on each breast. Black mohair braid all round body forming barrels (or dummies) at the bottom of the back seams. Collar of scarlet cloth, with ¼-inch braid all round with tracing braid all round inside forming an eye at each corner.	Rifle green cloth with double ⅜th inch black mohair braid stripes on a scarlet ground with light between the stripes.	Scarlet cloth, no collar, hooked up to the throat. Edged all round with black mohair tracing braid and a row of eyes behind forming a small Austrian knot at bottom of the vest. Two pockets edged with black tracing braid forming a crows foot at the end and above and below the centre.	Rifle green cloth with black mohair band and a black welt round the crown.

APPENDIX X—contd.

Details of mess dress and forage caps for Indian Pioneers and infantry—contd.

Unit.	Jacket.	Overalls.	Waistcoat.	Forage cap.
14th Punjab Regiment	Pointed cuffs of scarlet cloth with 1-inch mohair braid 6-inch deep from bottom of cuff with tracing braid above and below forming three eyes at the outer and one at the inner point. Shoulder straps of black chain gimp, hussar pattern. Badges of rank in black metal. Scarlet cloth. The jacket, cuffs, collar, and shoulder straps edged with white piping. Roll collar of green cloth. Pointed cuffs of green cloth, 6-inch deep at the points and 2¾ inches behind. 1-inch slit at the seams. Two buttons on each cuff. Shoulder straps of green cloth, 1¾-inch wide at the base tapering to about 1-inch at the points; rounded points fastened with a small button; sewn in at the shoulder. Badges of rank in metal.	Blue cloth with a scarlet welt ¼-inch wide down the side seams.	Green cloth, open in front, no collar, fastened with four vest buttons.	Blue cloth, with black oakleaf lace band and a scarlet welt round the crown.
15th Punjab Regiment (except 2nd Battalion).	Scarlet cloth. Roll collar of buff cloth. Pointed cuffs of buff cloth, 6 inches deep at the points and 2¾ inches behind. 1-inch slit at the seams. Shoulder straps of buff cloth, 1¾-inch wide at the base tapering to about 1 inch at the points; rounded points fastened with a small button; sewn in at the shoulder. Badges of rank in metal.	Ditto	Scarlet cloth, open in front, no collar, fastened with four vest buttons.	Ditto.

Appendices.

2nd Battalion, 15th Punjab Regiment.	Drab cloth, lined drab silk, fastened at the neck with a loop. Jacket is edged with drab mohair braid all round the body, forming barrels or dummies at the bottom of the back seams. Back seams trimmed with a double row of ½-inch mohair braid, forming a crow's foot at the top and finishing over the barrels or dummies at the bottom. Pockets trimmed with ½-inch mohair braid forming a crow's foot at each end and in the centre. Five waved loops of square cord in front with four rows of knitted olivets, two olivets on each loop. Collar and cuffs of scarlet cloth. The collar has half-inch mohair braid all round trimmed through the centre with plumes and a row of small eyes along the top edge. The cuffs are pointed with one-inch mohair braid with tracing of drab Russia braid forming a row of small eyes on the outside and the inside of the cuffs, and extending 6½-inch from the bottom of the cuffs. Shoulder straps of Hussar pattern in drab. Badges of rank in silver embroidery.	Drab cloth with a single 2-inch drab mohair braid stripe down the side seams.	Scarlet cloth, no collar, open half way down, fastened with hooks and eyes. Trimmed with ½-inch mohair braid on edges with ¼-inch braid down the front, one-inch from the edge. Pockets trimmed with ¼-inch mohair braid forming a crow's foot at each end.
16th Punjab Regiment	Scarlet cloth, 4 buttons down the front of the jacket. The jacket, cuffs, collar and shoulder straps edged with white piping. Roll collar of white cloth. Pointed cuffs of white cloth, 6 inches deep at the points and 2¼ inches behind. Two buttons on each cuff. 1 inch slit at the seams. Shoulder straps of white cloth, 1¾-inch wide at the base tapering to about 1 inch at the points; rounded points fastened with a small button and sewn in at the shoulder. Badges of rank in metal.	Blue cloth with a scarlet welt ¼ inch wide down the side seams.	White washing, open in front, no collar, fastened with four vest buttons.
			Ditto.

APPENDIX X—contd.

Details of mess dress and forage caps for Indian Pioneers and infantry—contd.

Unit.	Jacket.	Overalls.	Waistcoat.	Forage cap.
17th Dogra Regiment.	Scarlet cloth. The jacket, cuffs, collar and shoulder straps edged with white piping. Roll collar of yellow cloth. Pointed cuffs of yellow cloth, 6 inches deep at the points and 2¼ inches behind. Two buttons on each cuff. 1 inch slit at the seams. Shoulder straps of yellow cloth, 1⅜-inch wide at the base tapering to about 1 inch at the points; rounded points fastened with a small button and sewn in at the shoulder. Badges of rank in metal.	Blue cloth with a scarlet welt ¾ inch wide down the side seams.	Red cloth, open in front, no collar, fastened with four vest buttons.	Blue cloth, with black oakleaf lace band and a scarlet welt round the crown.
18th Royal Garhwal Rifles.	Rifle green cloth, with stand up collar fastened at the neck with a loop of braid at the bottom of the collar. Body trimmed with 1½-inch black mohair braid all round, forming barrels (or dummies) at the bottom of the back seams. Back seams trimmed with a double row of ¼ inch mohair braid forming a crow's foot at the top and finishing over the barrels (or dummies) at the bottom. Five waved loops of square cord in front two oviilettes on each loop double row of piping ¾ inch wide all round body, ¼ inch from the braid. A trimming of ¼ inch mohair braid forming four crows' feet on either side of the body under the arms.	Rifle green cloth with a single 2-inch black braid stripe down the side seams.	Rifle green cloth, no collar, open half way down, fastened with hooks and eyes. Trimmed with ¼ inch mohair braid on the edges with ¼ inch braid down the front 1 inch from the edge. Pockets trimmed with ¼ inch mohair braid forming a crow's foot at each end.	Rifle green cloth with black mohair braid band and a black welt round the crown.

Appendices.

	Collar of black velvet with mohair braid all round trimmed through the centre with plumes and a row of small eyes along the top edge. Pointed cuffs of black velvet with 1¾-inch mohair braid and tracing of black Russia braid forming a row of small eyes on the outside and inside of the cuffs, and extending 6¼-inch from the bottom of the cuff. Shoulder straps of black chain gimp, rifle regiment pattern.		
19th Hyderabad Regiment (except 1st Kumaon Rifles).	Scarlet cloth. The jacket, cuffs, collar and shoulder straps edged with white piping. Roll collar of rifle green cloth. Pointed cuffs of rifle green cloth, 6 inches deep at the points and 2¾ inches behind. 1 inch slit at the seams. Shoulder straps of rifle green cloth, 1¾ inches wide at the base tapering to about 1 inch at the points; rounded points fastened with a small button and sewn in at the shoulder. Badges of rank in metal.	Blue cloth with a scarlet welt ¼ inch wide down the side seams.	White washing, open in front, no collar, fastened with four vest buttons.	Blue cloth with black oakleaf lace band and a scarlet welt round the crown.
1st Kumaon Rifles	Rifle green cloth, with stand up collar fastened at the neck with a loop of braid at the bottom of the collar. Body trimmed with black mohair braid all round forming barrels (or dummies) at the bottom of the back seams. Back seams trimmed with a double row of ¼ inch mohair braid forming a crow's foot at the top and finishing over the barrels (or dummies) at the bottom. Five waved loops of square cord in front with four knitted olivets, two olivets on each loop. Pockets trimmed with ¼ inch mohair braid forming a crow's foot at each end and in the centre.	Rifle green cloth with a single 2-inch black braid stripe down the side seams.	Rifle green cloth, no collar, open half way down fastened with hooks and eyes. Trimmed with ¼ inch mohair braid on the edges with ¼ inch braid down the front, 1 inch from the edge. Pockets trimmed with ½ inch mohair braid forming a crow's foot at each end.	Rifle green, with black mohair band and a black welt round the crown.

E

APPENDIX X—contd.

Details of mess dress and forage caps for Indian Pioneers and infantry—contd.

Unit.	Jacket.	Overalls.	Waistcoat.	Forage cap.
20th Burma Rifles	Rifle green cloth Roll collar of rifle green cloth. Pointed cuffs of scarlet cloth, 6 inches deep at the points and 2¾ inches behind. 1 inch slit at the seams. Shoulder straps of rifle green cloth, 1¾-inch wide at the base tapering to about 1 inch at the points; rounded points fastened with a small button and sewn in at the shoulder. Badges of rank in black metal.	Rifle green cloth with a single 2-inch black braid stripe down the side seams.	Rifle green cloth, open in front, no collar, fastened with four vest buttons.	black mohair braid band and a black welt round the crown.
1st K. G. O. Gurkha Rifles.	Collar of black cloth with ¼ inch mohair braid all round trimmed through the centre with plume and a row of small eyes along the top edge. Pointed cuffs of black cloth with 1 inch mohair braid and tracing of black Russia braid forming a row of small eyes on the outside and inside of the cuffs, and extending 6½ inches from the bottom of the cuff. Shoulder straps of black chain gimp, rifle regiment pattern. Badges of rank in black metal. Rifle green cloth, with stand up collar fastened at the neck with a loop of braid at the bottom of the collar. Body trimmed with black mohair braid all round, forming barrels (or dummies) at the bottom of the back seams. Back seams trimmed with a double row of ¼ inch mo-	Rifle green cloth, with 2-inch black braid down the side seams.	Rifle green cloth, no collar, open half way down, fastened with hooks and eyes. Trimmed with ¼ inch mohair braid on the edges with ¼ inch braid down the front, 1 inch from the edge.	Ditto.

Appendices.

2nd K. E. O. Gurkha Rifles.	hair braid forming a crow's foot at the top and finishing over the barrels (or dummies) at the bottom. Five waved loops of square cord in front with four rows of knitted olivets, two olivets on each loop. Collar of scarlet cloth with ¼ inch mohair braid all round trimmed through the centre with plumes and a row of small eyes along the top edge. Pointed cuffs of scarlet cloth with 1 inch mohair braid and tracing of black Russia braid forming a row of small eyes on the outside and inside of the cuffs, and extending 6¼ inches from the bottom of the cuff. Shoulder straps of black chain gimp, rifle regiment pattern. Pockets trimmed with ¼ inch mohair braid forming a crow's foot at each end and in the centre. Badges of rank in black metal.	Rifle green cloth with a single 2-inch black braid stripe down the side seams.	Pockets trimmed with ¼ inch mohair braid forming a crow's foot at each end.
	Rifle green cloth Roll collar of rifle green cloth. Pointed cuffs of scarlet cloth, 6 inches deep at the points and 2¼ inches behind, trimmed with 1 inch black mohair braid and tracing braid. 1 inch slit at the seams. No shoulder straps. Badges of rank in black metal.		Rifle green cloth, open in front, no collar, fastened with four vest buttons.	Rifle green cloth with red and black dice board pattern band and a black welt round the crown.
3rd Q. A. O. Gurkha Rifles.	Rifle green cloth, with stand up collar fastened at the neck with a loop of braid at the bottom of the collar. Body trimmed with black mohair braid all round forming barrels (or dummies) at the bottom of the back seams. Back seams trimmed with a double row of ¼ inch mohair braid forming a crow's foot at the top and finishing over the barrels (or dummies) at the bottom. Five waved loops of square cord in front with four rows of knitted olivets, two olivets on each loop.	Rifle green cloth with 2-inch black braid stripes.	Rifle green cloth, no collar, open half way down, fastened with hooks and eyes. Trimmed with ¼ inch mohair braid on the edges with ¼ inch braid down the fronts 1 inch from the edges. Pockets trimmed with ¼-inch mohair braid forming a crow's foot at each end.	Rifle green cloth with black mohair band and a black welt round the crown.

E 2

APPENDIX X—contd.

Details of mess dress and forage caps for Indian Pioneers and infantry—contd.

Unit.	Jacket.	Overalls.	Waistcoat.	Forage cap.
4th P. W. O. Gurkha Rifles.	Rifle green cloth, with stand up collar fastened at the neck with a loop of braid at the bottom of the collar. Body trimmed with black mohair braid all round, forming barrels (or dummies) at the bottom of the back seams. Back seams trimmed with a double row of ¼ inch mohair braid forming a crow's foot at the top and finishing over the barrels (or dummies) at the bottom. Five waved loops of square cord in front with four rows of knitted olivetes, two olivetes on each loop. Pockets trimmed with ¼ inch mohair braid forming a crows foot at each end and in the centre. Pockets trimmed with ¼ inch mohair braid forming a crow's foot at each end and in the centre. Collar of black velvet with ¾ inch mohair braid all round trimmed through the centre with plumes and a row of small eyes along the top edge. Pointed cuffs of black velvet with 1-inch mohair braid and tracing of black Russia braid forming a row of small eyes on the outside and inside of the cuffs and extending 6½ inches from the bottom of the cuffs. Shoulder straps of black chain gimp, rifle regiment pattern. Badges of rank in black metal.	Rifle green cloth with 2-inch black braid down the seams.	Rifle green cloth, no collar, open half way down, fastened with hooks and eyes. Trimmed with ¼ inch mohair braid on the edges with ¼ inch braid down the fronts 1 inch from the edges. Pockets trimmed with ¼-inch mohair braid forming a crow's foot at each end.	Rifle green cloth with black mohair band and a black welt round the crown.

Appendices. 97

5th Royal Gurkha Rifles (Frontier Force).	Collar of black velvet with ¾ inch mohair braid all round trimmed through the centre with plumes and a row of small eyes along the top edge. Pointed cuffs of black velvet with 1 inch mohair braid and tracing of black Russia braid forming a row of small eyes on the outside and inside of the cuffs, and extending 6¼ inches from the bottom of the cuff. Shoulder straps of black chain gimp, rifle regiment pattern. Badges of rank in black metal.	Rifle green cloth with a single 2-inch mohair braid stripe down the side seams.	Rifle green cloth, open in front, no collar, fastened with four vest buttons.	Rifle green cloth with black mohair band and a black welt round the crown.
6th Gurkha Rifles	Rifle green cloth Roll collar of black silk. Pointed cuffs of black cloth, 6-inch deep at the points and 2½-inch behind, 1-inch slit at the seams. Shoulder straps of rifle green cloth, 1¾-inch at the base tapering to about 1 inch at the points; rounded points fastened with a small button, and sewn in at the shoulder. Badges of rank in black metal.	Ditto .	Ditto .	Ditto.
7th Gurkha Rifles	Rifle green cloth, with stand up collar fastened at the neck with a loop of braid at the bottom of the collar. Body trimmed with black mohair braid all round, forming barrels (or dummies) at the bottom of the back seams. Back seams trimmed with a double row of ¼ inch	Rifle green cloth with 2-inch black braid down the side seams.	Rifle green cloth, no collar, open half way down, fastened with hooks and eyes. Trimmed with ¼ inch mohair braid on the edges with ¼ inch braid down the front, 1 inch from the edge.	Ditto.

APPENDIX X—contd.

Details of mess dress and forage caps for Indian Pioneers and infantry—contd.

Unit.	Jacket.	Overalls.	Waistcoat.	Forage cap.
	mohair braid forming a crow's foot at the top and finishing over the barrels (or dummies) at the bottom. Five waved loops of square cord in front with four rows of knitted olivets, two olivets on each loop. Pockets trimmed with ¼ inch mohair braid forming a crow's foot at each end and in the centre. Collar of black velvet with ½ inch mohair braid all round trimmed through the centre with plumes and a row of small eyes along the top edge. Pointed cuffs of black velvet with 1 inch mohair braid and tracing of black Russia braid forming a row of small eyes on the outside and inside of the cuffs, and extending 6½ inches from the bottom of the cuff. Shoulder straps of black chain gimp, rifle regiment pattern. Badges of rank in black metal.		Pockets trimmed with ¼ inch mohair braid forming a crow's foot at each end.	
8th Gurkha Rifles	Rifle green cloth, with stand up collar fastened at the neck with a loop of braid at the bottom of the collar. Body trimmed with black mohair braid all round, forming barrels (or dummies) at the bottom of the back seams. Back seams trimmed with a double row of ¼ inch mohair braid forming a crow's foot at the top and finishing over the barrels (or dummies) at the bottom. Five waved	Rifle green cloth with a single 2-inch black braid stripe down the side seams.	Rifle green cloth, no collar, open half way down, fastened with hooks and eyes. Trimmed with ½ inch mohair braid on the edges with ¼ inch braid down the front, 1 inch from the edge. Pockets trimmed with ¾ inch mohair braid forming a crow's foot at each end.	Rifle green cloth with black mohair band and a black welt round the crown.

Appendices.

9th Gurkha Rifles	Rifle green cloth Roll collar of black silk. Pointed cuffs of rifle green cloth, 6 inches deep at the points and 2¾ inches behind, 1-inch slit at the seams. Shoulder straps of rifle green cloth, 1¾-inch at the base tapering to about 1-inch at the points, fastened with a small buttons, sewn in at the shoulder. Badges of rank in black metal.	Rifle green cloth with a single 2-inch mohair braid stripe down the side seams.	Rifle green cloth, open in front, no collar, fastened with four vest buttons.
10th Gurkha Rifles	Rifle green cloth, with stand up collar fastened at the neck with a loop of braid at the bottom of the collar. Body trimmed with black mohair braid all round forming barrels (or dummies) at the bottom of the back seams. Back seams trimmed with a double row of ¼ inch mohair braid forming a crow's foot at the top and finishing over the barrels (or dummies) at the bottom. Five waved loops of square cord in front with four rows of knitted olivets, two olivets on each loop. Pockets trimmed with ¼ inch mohair braid forming a crow's foot at each end and in the centre. Collar of black velvet with ½ inch mohair braid all round trimmed through the centre with plumes and a row of small eyes along the top edge. Pointed cuffs of black velvet with 1 inch mohair braid and tracing of black Russia braid forming a row of small eyes on the outside and inside of the cuffs, and extending 6¼ inches from the bottom of the cuff. Shoulder straps of black chain gimp, rifle regiment pattern. Badges of rank in black metal.	Rifle green cloth with a single 2-inch black braid stripe down the side seams.	Rifle green cloth, no collar, open half way down, fastened with hooks and eyes. Trimmed with ½ inch mohair braid on the edges with ¼ inch braid down the fronts 1 inch from the edges. Pockets trimmed with ¼ inch mohair braid forming a crow's foot at each end.

APPENDIX X—*contd.*

Details of mess dress and forage caps for Indian Pioneers and infantry—*concld.*

Unit.	Jacket.	Overalls.	Waistcoat.	Forage cap.
	loops of square cord in front with four rows of knitted olivets, two olivets on each loop. Pockets trimmed with ½ inch mohair braid forming a crow's foot at each end and in the centre. Collar of black velvet with ½ inch mohair braid all round trimmed through the centre with plumes and a row of small eves along the top edge. Pointed cuffs of black velvet with 1 inch mohair braid and tracing of black Russia braid forming a row of small eyes on the outside and inside of the cuffs and extending 6½ inches from the bottom of the cuffs. Shoulder straps of black chain gimp rifle regiment pattern. Badges of rank in black metal.			

APPENDIX XI.

Badges and devices of Indian infantry.

Regiment.	On buttons.	On collar of tunic and mess jacket.	On collar of service dress.	On head-dress (helmet, pagri, or felt hat).	On cap.
Corps of Madras Pioneers.	In gilding metal, crossed axes encircled by the words "MADRAS PIONEERS."	Crossed pick axe and shovel surmounted by an elephant. *Special additional badge to be worn on the lapel of the mess jacket by the 1st (King George's Own) Battalion.* "The Cypher of His Majesty King George V."	As on collar of tunic and mess jacket.	*Helmet.* No badge. *Pagri.* An elephant on a flat scroll inscribed "Assaye". The whole within a band inscribed "SEETA BULDEE SERINGAPATAM" in the upper half. Placed on the lower portion of the band but within it and immediately below "ASSAYE", a crossed pick axe and shovel. The band surmounted by a crown and below the band a scroll inscribed "CORPS OF MADRAS PIONEERS."	As on collar of tunic and mess jacket.
Corps of Bombay Pioneers.	In gilding metal crossed felling axes. In upper angle a mural crown.	In silver crossed axes.	In silver as on collar of tunic and mess jacket.	*Nil*	In silver, crossed felling axes. In upper angle a mural crown.
Corps of Sikh Pioneers	In brass crossed felling axes, surmounted by an Imperial Crown. (Size of all buttons, *i.e.*, front pocket and shoulder straps 24 lines and the button to have a raised edge).	On collar of mess jacket only. In silver, crossed axes.	*Nil*	In silver a quoit bearing the words "SIKH PIONEERS". Above the quoit a crown. Below the quoit a scroll bearing the corps motto "AUT VIAM INVENIAM AUT FACIAM".	Same as on helmet but smaller.

APPENDIX XI—contd.

Badges and devices of Indian infantry—contd.

Regiment.	On buttons.	On collar of tunic and mess jacket.	On collar of service dress.	On head-dress (helmet, pagri, or felt hat).	On cap.
Corps of Hazara Pioneers.	In scarlet uniform, plain brass buttons. In other kit plain white metal buttons. *For mess waistcoat.*—In silver, crossed axes in gold.	As for cap, only smaller.	*Nil*	*Nil*	In silver, crossed axes with a crown in upper angle; below a scroll inscribed "HAZARA PIONEERS".
1st Punjab Regiment	In brass, a distorted dragon wearing an Imperial crown. *Mess waistcoat button.*—On gilt, in silver, "1" with a small scroll in centre surrounded by a laurel wreath and surmounted by a Crown.	In silver, an elephant, on a rectangular tablet inscribed "ASSAYE."	*Service dress (drill).*—In brass, as on collar of tunic and mess jacket. *Service dress (serge).*—In bronze, as on collar of tunic and mess jacket.	*On helmet.*—As on forage cap.	*Forage cap.*—A silver elephant on a rectangular tablet inscribed "ASSAYE" below a silver dragon wearing an Imperial Crown. The elephant surmounted by a silver semi-circular scroll inscribed "1st PUNJAB REGIMENT" above a crown in brass. The whole on a brass star with rays as in the Star of India. *On F. S. cap.*—A dragon in brass

					wearing an Imperial crown below, on right, between dragon's forefeet, a small silver scroll inscribed "CHINA" below a silver scroll inscribed "1st PUNJAB REGIMENT."
2nd Punjab Regiment (1st, 2nd, 3rd, 5th and 10th battalions only).	In gilding metal in Arabic "2" surmounted by an Imperial Crown, the word "Punjab" at the top, and the word "Regiment" below, in the form of a circle. *Mess dress buttons.*—A gilt button with a silver galley.	A galley, in gold braid. *On white mess jacket.*—A galley in silver.	*Nil.*	*Nil*	*On forage cap.*—A galley in gold braid. *On service dress cap.*—A bronze galley with a scroll below inscribed "2nd Punjab Regiment."
2nd Punjab Regiment (4th battalion only).	In gilding metal, an Arabic "2" surmounted by an Imperial Crown, the word "Punjab" at the top, and the word "Regiment" below, in the form of a circle. *Mess dress buttons.*—In gilt a dragon.	*Tunic.*—An embroidered dragon (gold on green). *Mess jacket.*—A metal dragon.	*Nil*	A metal dragon	*On forage cap.*—An embroidered dragon (gold on green). *On service dress cap.*—A metal dragon.
4th Bombay Grenadiers.	Brass button stamped with a grenade. *Mess waistcoat button.*—Flat silver button with gilt grenade.	*British and Indian officers only.*—A gold embroidered grenade with the figure "4" in silver.	A brass grenade with the figure "4" in white metal.	*British and Indian officers only.*—A brass grenade with the figure "4" in white metal.	A gold embroidered grenade with the figure "4" in silver.

APPENDIX XI—*contd*

Badges and devices of Indian infantry—*contd*.

Regiment.	On buttons.	On collar of tunic and mess jacket.	On collar of service dress.	On head-dress (helmet, pagri, or felt hat).	On cap.
		Special additional badge to be worn on the lapel of the mess jacket above the regimental badge by the 2nd Battalion (King Edward's Own).—The Cypher of King Edward VII.		*Indian other ranks.*—A brass grenade (no number). *Special badge to be worn in front of the full dress head-dress by the 2nd Battalion (King Edward's Own).*—The Cypher of King Edward VII.	
5th Mahratta Light Infantry.	In silver, placed in relief on a gilding metal button, a bugle surmounted by a crown with "5", between the strings.	In silver, a bugle surmounted by a crown with "5" between the strings.	*Nil*	*Nil*	As on collar of tunic and mess jacket, but larger.
6th Rajputana Rifles.	In black horn, a bugle surmounted by a crown.	*On collar of mess jacket only.*—In silver, crossed katars. *Note.*—A pair consists of one badge with left katar crossed over right katar, and one badge with right katar crossed over left katar.	*Nil*	*Nil*	In silver, on a red boss a bugle.

7th Rajput Regiment	*British and Indian officers only.*—In gilding metal "VII," surmounted by a crown with a scroll below inscribed "Rajputs." *Mess dress buttons.*—In silver, placed in relief on a flat gilt button "VII" surrounded by six pointed leaves with the stalks held by a band containing oak leaves and acorns. Above the Royal Crest; and below, a scroll inscribed "Rajput Regiment."	*Special additional badge to be worn on the lapel of the mess jacket above the regimental badge by the 2nd Battalion (Prince of Wales' Own).*—The plume of His Royal Highness the Prince of Wales. *On collar of mess jacket.*—Single silver katar. *Special additional badges to be worn on the lapel of the mess jacket above the regimental badge by:—* *1st Battalion (Queen Victoria's Own Light Infantry).*—The Cypher of Queen Victoria. *2nd Battalion (Prince Albert Victor's).*—The letters "P. A. V.," in monogram, surmounted by a crown. *3rd Battalion (Duke of Connaught's Own).*—The Cypher of His Royal Highness the Duke of Connaught.	*Special badge to be worn in front of the full dress head-dress by the 2nd Battalion (Prince of Wales' Own).*—The plume of His Royal Highness the Prince of Wales. *Nil* *In gilt for British and Indian officers and brass for Indian ranks.*—"VII" surrounded by six pointed leaves with the stalks held by a band containing oak leaves and acorns. Above the Royal Crest; and below, a scroll inscribed "Rajput Regiment." *Special badges to be worn in front of the full dress head-dress by:—* *1st Battalion (Queen Victoria's Own Light Infantry).*—The Cypher of Queen Victoria. *2nd Battalion (Prince Albert Victor's).*—The letters "P. A. V." in monogram, surmounted by a crown. *3rd Battalion (Duke of Connaught's Own).*—The Cypher of His Royal Highness the Duke of Connaught.	In silver, as on head-dress, but smaller.

APPENDIX XI—contd.

Badges and devices of Indian infantry—contd.

Regiment.	On buttons.	On collar of tunic and mess jacket.	On collar of service dress.	On head-dress (helmet, pagri, or felt hat).	On cap.
8th Punjab Regiment	"8" on a plain gilding metal button. *For mess jacket.*—"8" on a plain silver button. *For mess waistcoat.*—Small silver button with The Chinthe embossed.	In silver, The Chinthe. *Special additional badge to be worn on the lapel of the mess jacket above the regimental badge by the 4th Battalion (Prince of Wales' Own).*—The plume of His Royal Highness the Prince of Wales.	Nil	In silver, on a blue patch. The Chinthe with a scroll below inscribed 8 "Punjab Regiment." *Special badge to be worn in front of the full dress head-dress by the 4th Battalion (Prince of Wales' Own).*—The plume of His Royal Highness the Prince of Wales.	In silver, as on head-dress.
9th Jat Regiment	Gilding metal buttons device as for tunic and mess jacket.	In silver, "IX" surmounted by a crown with "Jat Regiment" on a scroll below.	As on collar of tunic and mess jacket.	Nil	As on collar of tunic and mess jacket, but larger.
10th Baluch Regiment	*For British and Indian officers.*—Silver plain round ball buttons. *Indian ranks.*—White metal round ball buttons.	Nil *Special badges to be worn on the lapel of the mess jacket by :—* *1st Battalion (Duchess of Connaught's Own).*—The Cypher of Her Royal Highness the Duchess of Connaught. *3rd Battalion (Queen Mary's Own).*—The Cypher of Her Majesty Queen Mary.}	Nil	Nil *Special badges to be worn in front of the full dress head-dress by :—* *1st Battalion (Duchess of Connaught's Own).*—The Cypher of Her Royal Highness the Duchess of Connaught. *3rd Battalion (Queen Mary's Own).*—The Cypher of Her Majesty Queen Mary.	In silver on a cherry boss, the Roman figure "X".

Appendices. 107

Regiment	Buttons	Badges on collar of tunic	Badges on collar of mess jacket	Other badges
(continued from previous page)		4th Battalion (Duke of Connaught's Own).—The Cypher of His Royal Highness the Duke of Connaught. 5th Battalion (King George's Own). (Jacob's Rifles).—The Cypher of His Majesty King George V.	As on collar of tunic.	As on collar of tunic but larger.
11th Sikh Regiment (Except 1st and 3rd Battalions).	Brass button with raised quoit surmounted by a crown. In the centre of the quoit the word "Sikhs."	Plain silver quoit. Special additional badges to be worn on the lapel of the mess jacket above the regimental badge by the 5th Battalion (Duke of Connaught's Own).—The Cypher of His Royal Highness the Duke of Connaught.	As on collar of tunic.	As on collar of tunic but larger. Special badges to be worn in front of the full dress head-dress by the 5th Battalion (Duke of Connaught's Own).—The Cypher of His Royal Highness the Duke of Connaught. 4th Battalion (Duke of Connaught's Own).—The Cypher of His Royal Highness the Duke of Connaught. 5th Battalion (King George's Own). (Jacob's Rifles).—The Cypher of His Majesty King George V.
1st Battalion (King George's Own) (Ferozepore Sikhs).	As above	In silver a quoit above the plumes of His Royal Highness the Prince of Wales. Feathers and scroll in silver and crown in gilt.	As on collar of tunic and mess jacket.	*Indian officers and other ranks.*—In silver the plumes of His Royal Highness the Prince of Wales. Feathers and scroll in silver and crown in gilt.
3rd Battalion (Rattray's Sikhs).	As above	In silver a quoit with a dagger.	As on collar of tunic and mess jacket.	*British officers on helmet.*—As on collar of tunic and mess jacket but larger. *Indian officers and other ranks.*—As for British officers but larger and of steel.
12th Frontier Force Regiment.	Plain white metal buttons	On the collar of the tunic of all battalions except the 5th, and the collar of the	*Nil*	Special badge to be worn by the 1st Battalion (Prince of Wales' Own) (Sikhs) 1st, 2nd, 3rd and 4th battalions only.—The regimental badge.

APPENDIX XI—contd.

Badges and devices of indian infantry—contd.

Regiment.	On buttons.	On collar of tunic and mess jacket.	On collar of service dress.	On head-dress (helmet, pagri, or felt hat).	On cap.
		hot weather mess jacket of the 1st battalion, only.—in silver "12" within a stringed bugle and surmounted by a crown with a scroll on either side of the bugle inscribed "F. F." and "REGT" respectively. *Special additional badge to be worn on the collar of the hot weather mess jacket above the regimental badge by the 1st Battalion (Prince of Wales' Own) (Sikhs).*—In silver, the plume of His Royal Highness the Prince of Wales. *On the collar of the tunic of the 5th Battalion (Queen Victoria's Own Corps of Guides).*—The cypher of Queen Victoria within a Garter inscribed "HONI SOIT QUI MAL Y PENSE", and surmounted by a crown. The whole surrounded by a scroll bear-		*in the front of the full head dress.* In silver, the plume of the Prince of Wales.	*5th battalion only.*—In silver, the cypher of Queen Victoria, within a Garter inscribed "HONI SOIT QUI MAL Y PENSE", surmounted by a crown. The whole surrounded by a scroll bearing the words "Queen Victoria's Own Corps of Guides."

Appendices. 109

13th Frontier Force Rifles.	In black horn, a bugle surmounted by a crown. ing the words "Queen Victoria's Own Corps of Guides." *On collar of mess jacket only.*—In silver, a stringed bugle surmounted by a crown. Between the strings, in monogram, the figures and letters "13 F. F. R."	*Nil*	*Nil*	As on collar of mess jacket but larger.
14th Punjab Regiment	In gilding metal, a five-pointed star with a small ball at each re-entrant. In the centre of the star a circle and within the circle "14" on a frosted ground. The star surmounted by a Tudor Crown and below a scroll inscribed "PUNJAB REGIMENT." *Mess vest button.*—On a plain flat gilding metal button in mounted design a silver five pointed star with a small ball at each re-entrant. In the centre of the star a circle and within the circle "14" on a frosted ground.	In silver, a five pointed star with a small ball at each re-entrant. In the centre of the star a circle and within the circle "14" on a frosted ground. The star surmounted by a crown and below a scroll inscribed "PUNJAB REGIMENT." *Special additional badge to be worn on the lapel of the mess jacket above the regimental badge by the 2nd Battalion (Duke of Cambridge's Own) (B r o w n l o w's).*—The Cypher of His Royal Highness the Duke of Cambridge.	*Nil*	*Forage cap.*—As for collar of tunic and mess jacket. *Service dress cap.*—As for collar of tunic and mess jacket but in bronze.
		Special badge to be worn in front of the full dress head-dress by the 2nd Battalion (Duke of Cambridge's Own) (Brownlow's).—The Cypher of His Royal Highness the Duke of Cambridge.		
15th Punjab Regiment (Except 2nd and 3rd battalions).	On a brass button, "15 Punjab." *Mess waistcoat button.*—⅞″ ball in lacquered brass with "15" in frosted silver superimposed.	In brass, a quoit with frosted crescent interlaced. Above the quoit a crown.	As on collar of mess jacket.	*Nil*	In brass a quoit with frosted crescent interlaced. Above the quoit a crown. The whole encircled by a laurel wreath, and below a scroll inscribed "Punjab 15 Regiment."

APPENDIX XI—contd.

Badges and devices of Indian infantry—contd.

Regiment.	[On buttons.	On collar of tunic and mess jacket.	On collar of service dress.	On head-dress (helmet, pagri, or felt hat).	On cap.
2nd Battalion, 15th Punjab Regiment.	¾" ball plain white metal button. *Pocket button.*—⅝" ½-ball plain white metal.	In white metal, a quoit with frosted crescent interlaced, above the quoit a crown.	As on collar of mess jacket.	*Nil*	In white metal, crossed rifles with a bugle in the upper angle and the following below:— II. XV. Punjab Regiment.
3rd Battalion, 15th Punjab Regiment.	On a plain silver button, "XV." *Mess waistcoat button.*—On a small plain silver button, "XV."	In silver, the Royal and Imperial Cypher within the Garter and the motto "HONI SOIT QUI MALY PENSE." A Tudor crown above the whole encircled by a laurel wreath. Below a scroll inscribed "3rd Battalion 15th Punjab Regiment."	*Nil*	*Nil*	As on collar of mess jacket but larger.
16th Punjab Regiment	A plain cover gilding metal button with the figure "16" in the centre and the word "PUNJAB" below round the lower edge. *Mess vest button.*—Flat gilt button with slightly bevelled edges with "16" raised in silver in the centre.	In silver, a Maltese cross surmounted by a crown and encircled by a crescent. In the centre of the cross a quoit and within the quoit the figure "16." Below a scroll inscribed "PUNJAB REGIMENT."	*Nil*	*On helmet.*—As for collar of tunic and mess jacket but larger.	As for collar of tunic and mess jacket.

Appendices.

Regiment	Buttons	Collar badge	Pouch badge	Special badge	Helmet/Cap badge
17th Dogra Regiment	In gilding metal, "17" surmounted by a crown below a scroll inscribed "Dogras." *Mess waistcoat button.*—In silver, on a plain gilt button "17" surmounted by a crown with a scroll below inscribed "Dogras."	*Nil*	*Nil*	*Nil* / Special badge to be worn in front of the full dress head-dress by the 1st Battalion (Prince of Wales' Own).—The plume of His Royal Highness the Prince of Wales.	In silver "17" surmounted by a crown and a scroll below inscribed "Dogras."
18th Royal Garhwal Rifles	In black horn, a light infantry bugle with "R.G." within the strings: above a Tudor Crown.	In silver, a Maltese cross in the centre a stringed bugle within a band inscribed "ROYAL GARHWAL RIFLES," above a Tudor Crown.	*Nil*	*Nil* / Special badge to be worn on the lapel of the mess jacket by the 1st Battalion (Prince of Wales' Own).—The plume of His Royal Highness the Prince of Wales.	As on collar of tunic and mess jacket but larger and in bronze. / As on collar of tunic and mess jacket.
19th Hyderabad Regiment. 1st, 2nd, 3rd and 4th Battalions only.	On a gilding metal button in mounted design "XIX" surmounted by a crown. *Mess waistcoat button.*—A silver "XIX" placed in relief on a plain gilding metal button.	In silver, "XIX" surmounted by a crown, with a scroll below inscribed "Hyderabad Regiment."	As on collar of tunic and mess jacket.	*Nil*	*Nil*	As on collar of tunic and mess jacket.
1st Kumaon Rifles only.	In black horn, a stringed bugle with the letters "K. R." above.	In silver, a bugle.	*Nil*	*Nil*	*Nil*	In silver, on a green boss, a bugle with the letters "K. R." above.
20th Burma Rifles	In black horn, a bugle surmounted by a crown.	In silver, a peacock with a scroll below inscribed "BURMA RIFLES."	*Nil*	As on collar of tunic and mess jacket but larger.	As on collar of tunic and mess jacket.	
1st K. G. O. Gurkha Rifles (The Malaun Regiment).	In black horn, crossed khukris, edge downwards with "1" in upper angle and a stringed bugle in lower angle.	*Nil*	*Nil*	*On helmet.*—In oxidised silver crossed khukris with the plume of the Prince of Wales in the upper angle: in the lower angle a stringed bugle surmounted by the figure "1."	In silver, on a red boss, crossed khukris with the plume of the Prince of Wales in the upper angle: on the lower angle a stringed bugle surmounted by the figure "1."	

APPENDIX XI—contd.

Badges and devices of Indian infantry—contd.

Regiment.	On buttons.	On collar of tunic and mess jacket.	On collar of service dress.	On head-dress (helmet, pagri, or felt hat).	On cap.
2nd King Edward's Own Gurkha Rifles (The Sirmoor Rifles).	In black horn, crossed khukris edge downwards surmounted by the Royal and Imperial Cypher of King Edward VII.	*On white summer mess jacket.*—In silver, the plume of His Royal Highness the Prince of Wales.	Nil	*On white full dress helmet.*—In silver, the plume of His Royal Highness the Prince of Wales.	*On Kilmarnock cap.*—In silver, crossed khukris, edge downwards with the plume of the Prince of Wales in upper angle. The figure "1" below the centre of the coronet. The plume of His Royal Highness the Prince of Wales, in silver on a red boss. *On Kilmarnock cap for Gurkha ranks.*—The plume of His Royal Highness the Prince of Wales, in bronze.
3rd Q. A. O. Gurkha Rifles.	In black horn, crossed khukris, edge upwards with "3" in upper angle.	*On collar of mess jacket only.*—The Cypher of Queen Alexandra ensigned with the Imperial Crown.	Nil	*On felt hat.*—In black metal, the Cypher of Queen Alexandra ensigned with the Imperial Crown.	In silver, the Cypher of Queen Alexandra ensigned with the Imperial Crown. (On buttons in front two crossed khukris enclosing a "3" in silver.)

Appendices.

Regiment					
4th Prince of Wales' Own Gurkha Rifles.	In black horn, crossed khukris surmounted by the plume of His Royal Highness the Prince of Wales. In the lower angle of the kukris, the figure "IV."	In silver, the plume of His Royal Highness the Prince of Wales.	*Nil*	In bronze, crossed khukris surmounted by the plume of His Royal Highness the Prince of Wales. In the lower angle of the khukris, the figure "IV."	In silver, as on collar of tunic and mess jacket.
5th Royal Gurkha Rifles (Frontier Force).	In black horn crossed khukris with "5" in the upper angle, surmounted by the Royal Crest.	In silver, crossed khukris with "5" in the upper angle, surmounted by the Royal Crest.	*Nil*	As in column 3, to be worn on white full dress helmet (when worn).	As in column 3.
6th Gurkah Rifles	In black horn, crossed khukris, edge downwards and "6" between the handles.	In silver crossed khukris, edge downwards "6" between the handles.	*Nil*	*Nil*	In silver crossed khukris, edge downwards and "6" between the handles below a scroll inscribed "GURKHA RIFLES."
7th Gurkha Rifles	In black horn, crossed khukris, edge upwards with "7" in upper angle.	*Nil*	*Nil*	*On helmet.*—In silver crossed khukris, edge upwards with "7" in the upper angle.	In silver, as on holmet.
8th Gurkha Rifles	In black horn, crossed khukris with "8" in the upper angle.	In silver crossed khukris with "8" in the upper angle.	*Nil*	*Nil*	In silver, on a black bar as on collar of mess jacket.

On Kilmarnock cap.—In white metal, crossed khukris, edge upwards with "3" in upper angle surmounted by the Cypher of Queen Alexandra ensigned with the Imperial Crown.

APPENDIX XI—concld.

Badges and devices of Indian infantry—concld.

Regiment.	On buttons.	On collar of tunic and mess jacket.	On collar of service dress.	On head-dress (helmet, pagri, or felt hat).	On cap.
9th Gurkha Rifles	In black horn, crossed khukris, edge downward within lower angle.	In silver crossed khukris, with a crown in upper angle.	Nil	*On helmet.*—In silver, crossed edge downwards with "9" in lower angle.	In silver, on a black bar as on helmet.
10th Gurkha Rifles	In black horn, a bugle suspended by knotted strings crossed by a khukri, edge downwards.	*On collar openners jacket only.*—In silver, a bugle suspended by knotted strings crossed by a khukri, edge downwards.	Nil	*On helmet.*—Crossed khukris, edge downwards, and "15" in upper angle.	On forage cap (Gurkha officer, Kilmarnock cap).—In silver, as on helmet.

APPENDIX XII.

Units who have been permitted to adopt hot weather mess kit which differs from that shewn in para. 189.

Unit.	Detail of differences from the standard shewn in para. 189.
3rd Cavalry	White drill jacket with stand up collar. Open end sleeves fastened with two small buttons.
7th Light Cavalry	White drill jacket with stand up collar. Buttons on the right side. French grey piping in sleeves and down the back seams.
19th K. G. O. Lancers	White drill jacket with stand up collar. Dark blue Lancer piping.
20th Lancers	White drill jacket with stand up collar. French grey piping.
1st Battalion, 5th Mahratta Light Infantry.	White drill jacket with stand up collar.
11th Sikh Regiment	Thin red kashmir jacket with yellow facings.
1st, 2nd, 3rd, and 4th Battalions, 12th Frontier Force Regiment.	White drill jacket with stand up collar, fastened at the neck with a loop of white cord.
5th Battalion, 12th Frontier Force Regiment.	White drill jacket with stand up collar, fastened at the neck with a loop of white cord. Red piping round the jacket, collar and cuffs.
18th Royal Garhwal Rifles	White drill jacket with stand up collar. No collar badges.
10th Gurkha Rifles	Thin dark green serge with stand up collar. No braid on jacket. Shoulder straps same material as the jacket.
Corps of Madras Pioneers	White drill jacket with stand up collar fastened at the throat. Worn without a linen collar and dress tie.
The Hazara Pioneers	White drill jacket with stand up collar. Plume colour piping.

INDEX.

A

	Paras.
Aide-de-camp—	
Commander-in-Chief	90
General officers commanding	90
G. O's. C. in-chief	90
Indian to the Viceroy	100
King	83-87
Aiguillette—	
Indian orderlies to the King	89
Extra equerries to the Prince of Wales	89
General description	11
Staff and personal appointments	107
Appointments—	
Staff and personal	111-117
Armlets	116
Army in India Reserve of Officers—	
Mess dress	122-124, 196

B

	Paras.
Badges—	
Authorised only to be worn	14
Collar	14
Mess dress position of	14
Rank, Size of	13
Special	15
Badges and devices—	
Army Remount Department	179
British officers, Viceroy's Bodyguard	128
Chaplains	194
General List, Indian Army	126
Indian Army Ordnance Corps	173
Indian Army Service Corps	163
Indian cavalry units	App. IX
Indian Infantry units	App. XI
Indian Medical Service	166
Military Farms Department	182
Miscellaneous List	187
Miscellaneous Corps and Departments	187
Retired officers	197
Balls—	
Wearing of uniform at	6
Removal of the sword	16
Removal of spurs	50

	Paras.
Barrack Department	183-187
Belts, "Sam Browne"	17 and App. I
Boots—	
Ankle	18(a)
Butcher	18
Field	18(e)
Jacked	18(c)
Wellington	18
Breeches—	
Bedford cord	20
Khaki cord	22
Khaki drill	23
Knickerbocker	21
Buttons	19

C

	Paras.
Cap—	
Badges, Indian cavalry	App. IX
Badges, Indian infantry	App. XI
Badges, corps and departments	166, 173, 179, 182 and 187
Comforter	24
Covers	28
Field	25
Forage	26
Service dress	27
Cape	73
Cavalry (Indian)	153 & App. VIII
Chains, shoulder	48
Chaplains	194
Chin straps	38
Church parades	76
Civil employ	195
Cloaks and capes—	
Bodyguards, H. E. the Viceroy	
British Officers	128
Indian Officers	133
Bodyguard, Governor of Madras	135
Bodyguard, Governor of Bombay	141
Bodyguard, Governor of Bengal	146
Clothing depots, purchases from	57
Collar badges	14
Collars	29
Colonels Commandant, on the Staff and Substantive	117
Colonel of a regiment—dress of—	
when a general officer	8A
Committees and boards	76

(117)

	Paras.
Courts of enquiry	76
Courts martial duty	76
Covers, cap.	28

D

	Paras.
Decorations and medals—	
General instructions	58
Departments—	
Army Remount	174-179
Civil	
Judge Advocate-General	180-182
Military Accounts	180-182
Military Detention Corps	183-187
Military Farms	180-182
Indian Medical Service	164-166
Indian Army Ordnance Corps	167-173
Indian Army Service Corps	158-163
Military Engineer Service including Barrack, Public Works, Telegraph, and Sapper and Miners	183-187
Indian Medical Department	183-187
Miscellaneous List	183-187
Deviations—	
From patterns forbidden	1
Distinctive letters or numerals	49
Dress—	
All officers in a unit must be dressed alike	77
British army officers on the Indian establishment	127
Church parades	76
General officer officiating in a regimental capacity	8A
On board ship	80
Orders of	76
Drill order	76

E

Emblems—	
To be worn on the helmet	4
To denote the possession of certain bars	67
To denote mention in despatches	68
Entertainments	64
Equerries—	
King Emperor	84
Prince of Wales	84
Royal Family, members of	84
Escorts	

	Paras.
Evening dress—	
Miniature decorations and medals	69
Ex A. D. C. General and ex-A. D. C. to the King—	
Wearing of Royal Cypher, etc.	88
Extra equerries to the Prince of Wales	89

F

Fancy dress balls	6
Farms —	
Departmental commissioned officers	183-187
Officers	180
Field cap	25
Field glasses	76
Field Marshal	117
Field service (active service)	81
Forage cap—	
Army Remount Department	174
Chaplains	194
Covers	28
General List, I. A.	125
I. A. O. C.	167
I. A. S. C.	164
Indian cavalry	153
Indian infantry	155
Miscellaneous Corps and Departments	183
Foreign countries, uniform in	5
Foreign decorations and medals—	
General instructions	74
Frock coat—	
Indian A.'s D. C. to the Viceroy	160
Universal	30
Frock serge. A	31
Frock serge. B	32
Frog sword belt—	
Description	App. I
When worn	17
Full dress—	
B. O.'s Governors Body Guard—	
Bengal	146
Bombay	141
Madras	135
B. O.'s Viceroys Bodyguard	128
May be worn if in possession	10
Funerals	64

Index. 119

G
	Paras.
General List—	
Mess dress	117-124
Service dress	119-122
Badges and devices	126
General officers	110
Gloves	33
Gorget patches	34
Chaplains	194
Great coats—	
For general officers and substantive colonels.	36
Universal	35
Guards of honour	64

H
Haversacks	64
Headquarters—	
General Staff	100-106
Helmet—	
Badges, Indian cavalry	152
Badges, Indian infantry	159, 166 and 173
Badges, corps and departments	184, 190, 200, 209, 217 and 225
General instructions	38
Khaki	38
Honorary physicians and surgeons—	
King Emperor.	72-79
Viceroy	92
Horse furniture—	
Branches of the army	82
British officers—	
Governor's Bodyguard—	
Bengal	149
Bombay	144
Madras	138
Viceroy's Bodyguard	131
Hot weather uniform—	
Branches of the army	189
British officers—	
Governor's Bodyguard—	
Bengal	149
Bombay	144
Madras	138
Viceroy's Bodyguard	131

I
	Paras.
Indian Army Ordnance Corps	167-173
Indian Army Service Corps	158-163
Indian cavalry—	
Badges and devices	App. IX
Mess dress	App. VIII
Indian infantry—	
Badges and devices	App. XI
Mess dress	App. X
Indian medical—	
Department	183-187
Service	164-166
Indian officers—	
With King's commission	78
With Viceroy's commission	78
Governor's Bodyguard—	
Bengal	151
Bombay	145
Madras	140
Viceroy's Bodyguard	133
Inspections	76
Interviews official	76

J
Jackets—	
Service dress	39
Serge	40
Jhodpur breeches	23
Judge Advocate General's Department	180-182

K
Kamarabands	193
King's commission—Indian officers holding	78
Knots sword—	
Description	App. I
Method of wearing	52

L
Leave—	
Wearing of uniform on	5
Leggings—	
Description	41
Wearing of	18
Which differ from authorised colour	App. VII

	Paras.
Levees	76
Lungi—	
Wearing of, by British officers .	38
For Indian officers . . .	78

M

	Paras.
Madras Governor's—	
Bodyguard . . .	133
Personal appointments . .	105
Manoeuvres—	
Foreign countries . .	5
Marching order . . .	76
Medals, orders and decorations—	
Chaplains . . .	75
Emblems . . .	67
Mention in despatches .	68
Semi-knots . . .	65
Evening dress . . .	69
Foreign	74
Full dress . . .	60
How worn . . .	58
Insigna of Knights Grand Cross etc.	71
Mess dress . . .	61
Miniature . . .	59
Order in which worn . .	72
Great war medals . .	73
Orders of dress . .	76
Order of—	
The Garter . . .	70
The Thistle . . .	70
Position of —on the jacket	58, 63
Retired officers . .	66
Ribands—	
Emblems on . .	67
Foreign medals . .	64
Width . . .	64
Orders . . .	70
Without medals . .	63
Service dress . . .	62
Semi-knots . . .	65
Mess dress—	
Army Remount Department .	175
A. I. R. O. . . .	122-124
Bodyguards—	
Bengal . . .	148
Bombay . . .	143
Madras . . .	137
Viceroy's . . .	130
Boots	18(d)
Hot weather . . .	188

	Paras.
Mess dress—*contd.*	
General List, I. A. . .	121
Indian Army Ordnance Corps .	168
Indian Army Service Corps .	159
Indian cavalry 154 and App.	VIII
Indian departments . .	184
Indian infantry . 155 and App.	X
Indian Medical Service . .	165
Judge Advocate General's Department	180
Medals and orders . . 59 and	61
Mess order . . .	76
Military Accounts Department .	180
Military Farms Department .	180
Nursing Service for Indian troops hospitals	199
Officers of the I. A. not on the cadre of a unit . . .	124
On board ship . . .	80
Optional for—	
Departmental officers for whom an outfit allowance is not admissible 80, 162, 172, 178,	185
Warrant officers 162, 172, 178,	185
Personal appointments Viceroy 96 and	99
Q. A. M. N. S. I. . . .	198
Retired officers . . .	197
Wearing of Royal Cypher and crown	86
Mourning band . . .	42
Military secretaries—	
Commander in chief . .	90
G. O.'s. C. i.c. Commands .	90
G. O.'s. C. Districts . . .	90

N

	Paras.
Nursing services—	
For Indian troops hospitals .	199
Queen Alexandra's Military Nursing Service for India . .	198
Naval messes . . .	76

O

	Paras.
Obsolete garments, wearing of .	2
Officers—	
Civil employ . . .	19
Not on the cadre of a unit	180-18
Retired	19

Index.

	Paras.
Officers—*contd.*	
Staff	107
Unattached list	180-182
On the cadre of units	111
Orderlies, Indian, to the King Emperor	89
Orders, decorations and medals— See under Medals.	
Orders of dress	76
Orders and general instructions	1
Ordnance factories, purchases from	57
Other ranks	79

P

Patches, gorget	34
Patterns, authorised, deviation from forbidden	1
Personal appointments	83, 90, 91, 100, 103, 107
Physicians, honorary to the King Emperor	87
Pistol	App. II
Pith hats	38-A
Plain clothes	
On board ship	80
Poppies, wearing of in headdress	4
Plume	91
Private secretaries	91-103
Purchase from ordnance factories	57
Putties	43 and App. VII

Q

Queen Alexandra's Military Nursing Service in India	198

R

Rank badges	13
Regimental badges and devices (see under badges and devices)	
Remount Department	174-179
Reserve of Officers, Army in India—	
Uniform to be maintained	196
Mess dress for	124
Mess dress optional	196
Responsibility of officers to see that garments obtained by them are of sealed pattern	3
Retired officers	197
Revolver	App. II
Revolver case	App. I
Ribands medal (see under Medals).	
Riding school	76

S

	Paras.
Sam Browne sword belt	17 and App. I
Scabbards	App. IV, 51
Secretary, private	84-96
Secretary, military	83-84
Serge frock	31-32
Shabraque—	
Bodyguard, Governor of Madras	139
Bodyguard, H. E. the Viceroy—	
British officers	132
Indian officers	134
Semi-knots	65
Service dress, definition of	45
Shamrock	4
Ships, dress on	80
Shirts	46
Shorts	23-47
Shoulder chains	48
Shoulder cords and straps	49
Shoulder titles	49
Special emblems	4
Spectators at parades	8
Spurs	50
Staff—	
Administrative	107
General	107
Headquarters	107, 114
Officers entitled to wear distinctions	116
Personal Appointments—	
Governors of Madras, Bombay and Bengal	103
H. E. the Viceroy	91
Stars and orders—	
General instructions (see under Medals).	
Station boards	76
Straps—	
Chin	38
Foot	50
Shoulder	49
Surgeon to the King Emperor	83
Surgeon to the Viceroy	99
Sword belts	17
Sword knot	App. 1(a), 52
Swords—	
Belts	17
Description	App. IV
Knot	App. 1(a), 52
Slings	16
Wearing of	16, 51

	Paras.
T	
Telegraph Dept.	183
Ties—	
Mess dress	53
Service dress	53
Titles shoulder	49
Chaplains	194
A. I. R. O.	196
Trousers	54
U	
Unattached List—	
General List	117-125
Miscellaneous	180-182
Uniform—	
Duties, etc.	7
Hot weather	188
Officers, I. A., not on the cadre of a unit	180-182
Officers in civil employ	195
Undress—	
Evening for personal appointments Governors	104
Viceroy's Bodyguard	129
Governor's Bodyguard—	
Bengal	147
Bombay	142
Madras	136
V	
Viceroys—	
Bodyguard—	
Evening undress	129
Full dress	128

	Paras.
Viceroys—*contd.*	
Undress blue	129
Mess dress	130
Hot weather uniform	131
Horse furniture	132
Indian officers	133-134
Personal appointments to—	
Full dress	91
Undress scarlet	92
Undress blue	94
Evening undress	96
Horse furniture	98
Hot weather uniform	98
General instructions	99
Indian officers	100-102
W	
War medals, great war, order in which worn	73
Warrant officers	App. VI
Webley pistol	App. II
Web sword belt	17 and App. I
Water bottle	App. V
Waterproof	55
Wearing of uniform—	
Balls, fancy dress, at	6
Foreign countries, in	5
Foreign manœuvres, at	5
Leave, on	5
Special to India after leaving Indian limits	9
Wellington boots	18
Whistles	56
White mess dress	188

Table shewing the numbers of the paragraphs in the 1925 edition and the corresponding paragraphs in the present (1931) edition.

1925 edition.	1931 edition.	1925 edition.	1931 edition.	1925 edition.	1931 edition.	1925 edition.	1931 edition.
1	1	47	53	91	98	139	146
2	2	48	54	92	99	140	147
3	3	49	55	93	100	141	148
4	4	50	56	94	101	142	149
5	5	51	57	95	102	143	150
6	6	52	58	96	103	144	151
7	7	53	59	97	104	145	152
8	8	54	60	98	105	146	153
..	8A	55	61	99	106	147	154
9	9	56	62	100	107	148	154
10	10	57	63	101	108	149	154
11	11	..	64	102	109	150	154
12	12	..	65	103	110	151	App. VIII
13	13	..	66	104	111	152	App. IX
14	14	..	67	105	112	153	155
15	15	..	68	106	113	154	156
16	16	58	69	107	114	155	156
17	17	59	70	108	115	156	156
18	18	60	..	109	116	157	156
19	19	60A	..	110	117	158	App. X
20	20	61	..	111	118	159	App. XI
20A	21	62	62	112	119	160	155
21	22	..	71	113	120	161	App. X
21A	23	63	72	114	121	162	App. X
22	24	..	73	115	121	163	App. X
23	25	63A	74	116	121	164	156
24	26	..	75	117	121	165	App. X
25	27	64	76	118	122	166	App. XI
26	28	65	76	119A	123	167	155
27	29	66	77	119B	124	168	App. X
27A	30	67	78	119C	124	169	App. X
28	31	68	79	119D	124	170	App. X
..	32	69	80	119E	124	171	156
29	33	70	81	..	125	172	App. X
30	34	71	82	119F	126	173	App. XI
31	35	72	83	120	127	174	157
..	36	73	83	121	128	175	158
..	37	74	84	122	129	176	159
32	38	75	85	123	130	177	159
33	39	76	86	124	131	178	159
..	40	77	83	125	132	179	159
34	41	78	87	126	133	180	..
35	42	79	87	127	134	181	160
36	43	80	88	128	135	182	161
37	44	81	88	129	136	183	162
38	..	82	89	130	137	184	163
39	45	83	90	131	138	185	164
40	46	84	91	132	139	186	165
41	47	85	92	133	140	187	165
42	48	86	93	134	141	188	165
43	49	87	94	135	142	189	165
44	50	88	95	136	143	190	166
45	51	89	96	137	144	191	167
46	52	90	97	138	145	192	168

Table shewing the numbers of the paragraphs in the 1925 edition and the corresponding paragraphs in the present (1931) edition—*contd.*

1925 edition.	1931 edition.	1925 edition.	1931 edition.	1925 edition.	1931 edition.	1925 edition.	1931 edition.
193	168	207	177	221	184	235	194
194	168	208	178	222	184	236	194
195	168	209	179	223	185	237	194
196	169	210	180	224	186	238	194
197	170	211		225	187	239	194
198	171	212	121	226	188	240	194
199	172	213	to	227	189	241	194
200	173	214	124	228	190	242	194
201	174	215		229	191	243	194
202	175	216	181	230	192	244	194
203	175	217	182	231	193	245	195
204	175	218	183	232	194	246	196
205	175	219	184	233	194	247	197
206	176	220	184	234	194	248	198

www.ingramcontent.com/pod-product-compliance
Lightning Source LLC
Chambersburg PA
CBHW030418100426
42812CB00028B/3014/J